God's Payroll
Whose work is it anyway?

God's Payroll
Whose work is it anyway?

Neil Hood

Authentic
LIFESTYLE

First published in 2003 by Authentic Lifestyle
Reprinted 2004

10 09 08 07 06 05 04   8 7 6 5 4 3 2

Authentic Lifestyle is an imprint of Authentic Media
PO Box 300, Carlisle, Cumbria, CA3 0QS, UK
Box 1047, Waynesboro, GA 30830-2047, USA
www.paternoster-publishing.com

British Library Cataloguing in Publication Data
A catalogue record for this book is available from the British Library

ISBN 1-85078-475-2

Cover design by David Lund
Typeset by Temple Design
Printed in Great Britain by Bell and Bain Ltd, Glasgow

*For our grandchildren, Emily and Isla,
with our prayers that they will grow up
to know Jesus Christ as Lord*

Contents

Dedication   v
Preface   ix
Biographical note   xiv

PART ONE: GUIDING PRINCIPLES FOR OUR WORK

1. **Work, the Bible and You**   3
   Whose work is it anyway?: An introduction   4
   How do I relate to the secular view of work?   8
   What kind of relationship with work does the Bible presume?   10
   A warning and a challenge   14

2. **The Importance of Your Work in God's Eyes**   17
   What's so special about my work?   18
   Is God in my attitudes to work?   24
   The attitudes at work that God wants   26

PART TWO: KEEPING A PERSPECTIVE ON OUR WORK

3. **Making Sense of the World of Work**   33
   What paradoxes do we find in work?   34
   What's happening to work?   38
   Is there a Christian way of making sense of work?   41
   Making sense while being still   43

PART THREE: LEARNING THROUGH THE PRACTICE OF OUR WORK

4. **Danger – Christians at Work**   49
   What dangers?   50
   Applying New Age thinking to our work   51
   Failing to be a witness at work   54
   Making a god out of a career   58
   A matter of relationships   61

5 **Conflict and the World of Work**   65
   Christians, work and the world   66
   Conflict – with our colleagues   68
   Conflict – with our owner   75

6. **Discipleship at Work**   81
   Fresh thinking about my work   82
   What are the people I work with learning about Christ from me?   84
   ... and how do they learn?   90
   What difference has Jesus made so far in my work?   94

7. **Working at the Moral Edge**   99
   Why think of a moral edge?   100
   What should a Christian focus on?   105
   Everyday moral choices at work   110
   What does divine power in action look like?   113

8. **Living through a Work Crisis** **115**
   Working for God – but feeling excluded 116
   What do I do when the world of work bypasses me? 119
   Learning from Elijah's crisis 127

PART FOUR: PROGRESSING IN OUR WORK WITH GOD

9. **Working in Line with God's Plan** **135**
   Do I understand my call and its consequences? 136
   Do I create and take my opportunities? 142
   How much progress am I making? 147
   Asking questions, getting God's answers 149

10. **Weighing My Work in the Balance** **153**
   Whose work is it anyway?: Conclusion 154
   Whose scales am I using? 159
   Setting the course for the way ahead 163
   A final word 168

Preface

This is a book written by a fellow traveler through the world of work – not by an expert or a saint. Like you, I share in the trials and triumphs of work. Many of us spend a lot of time talking about our work, but we don't talk much about being a Christian at work. Indeed, for many Christians work almost seems to be a "no go" area – at least as it relates to our minds and our prayers. While we spend a great proportion of our lives at work, and although work dominates much of the rest of our lives, it is rarely the subject of church teaching. When the church does address the subject of work, many claim that its guidance is of little relevance in the "real" world of work in the twenty-first century. Thus the duality of being a Christian and being at work is born, fostered and fossilized. This is not the message of the Bible. Jesus never intended for us to have the inherent skepticism about the application of our faith to our work that some Christians display. Neither did he ask his followers to make a false distinction between secular and spiritual work.

However, I can personally relate to those who have concerns and confusions regarding work. I know many Christians who feel both anxious and guilty about their relationship with the world of work. Moreover, I share some of these feelings. Work is a topic that generates a whole spectrum of emotions. Satisfaction and frustration; fulfillment and boredom; preoccupation and indifference; liberation and exhaustion; clarity and confusion are among the many pairs of adjectives that describe my own experience. You probably share some of them and could add others as well. For some Christians, work is a constant source of anxiety, worry, stress and tension. For others, the dominant issue is that of work-life balance, or the lack thereof. Some Christians find their work constantly fulfilling and readily take its pressures in their stride. Others struggle with uncertainty over either the lack of employment or its terms and conditions. So, paradoxically, Christians with too much work experience some of the same emotions as those with too little work to meet their needs for self-satisfaction or income.

All of the above would be challenging enough, but there are other vital and often unanswered questions for the Christian. What does God expect from me in my work situation? How can I be a good witness in a job I hate? Am I in my job to please my employer or to please God? What kind of behavior distinguishes a faithful follower of Christ when he is heavily outnumbered at work? What do people I work with learn from me about Christ? And how do they learn? How do I handle conflict at work?

This book tackles these and many other related questions. Both the questions and the emotions that accompany them are part of my own daily work experience. This book reflects many years of wrestling with these issues, and I'm still traveling.

Why this book? This book is about Christian behavior both in and out of the world of work. I hope that you find it a "lived in" book that deals with real and pressing issues that you confront in your life – because I confront them in mine. This book begins on the sound biblical footing that although we may have disconnected our Christian practice from our work practice, God has not. We try to face work-related challenges daily, and even hourly, "without God", as it were – because the weekly sermon, the house group, the monthly seminar or the annual event planned to encourage us in our Christian lives all seem to be on an entirely different frequency. Yet the Lord has placed us in this real world of work, the principal context in which the majority of Christians are called to be salt and light, and he has not left us there on our own.

This book is the second in a series of books on Christian living, following *Whose Life Is It Anyway? A Lifeline in a Stress-Soaked World* (Carlisle: Authentic Lifestyle, 2002). *Whose Life Is It Anyway?* challenges Christians to respond to God's call for service. While God has a vast array of resources embedded in each of his disciples, he only uses a few of them because many are not "on offer". *Whose Life Is It Anyway?* examines many of the consequences of discipleship, touching briefly on the issue of work as one of the important realities of the Christian's life. The present volume specifically addresses the many different issues facing the Christian at work. While the two volumes can be read independently, in this book you will find occasional cross-references to matters discussed in *Whose Life Is It Anyway?* that are intended to be thought-provoking. As such, the two volumes complement each other.

While there are helpful books on the Christian at work, there are not many of them. Not surprisingly, it seems to have proved almost as difficult to write about work as it has been to deliver sermons about it. But this is a subject to which the church community – in every economic, cultural and political environment – needs to devote much more attention. We have to debunk the myths that secular work is divorced from, or less important than, church-based activity; that the ultimate aspiration of the Christian should be some form of "full-time" ministry; that the Bible has little of relevance to say to us on this subject, and so on. Having done that, the locus of our daily missionary activity becomes much clearer. I have little doubt that, for all of us, knowing the biblical answer to "Whose work is it anyway?" will provide uncomfortable challenges to the way we as Christians behave in our work environment.

Who is it for? This book is designed to be both practical and inclusive. The word "work" in the title refers principally (but not exclusively) to paid employment. Even that definition embraces many different relationships within the job market. So the issues covered here are of importance to the college student who works part-time in a coffee bar, to the senior citizen transporting disabled people to hospital on a part-time basis, to the senior executive in an international corporation and to the landscape gardener working outside his office window. This book is for Christians in every level of every profession. But it is also for those engaged in a range of other activities that may be entirely voluntary, as well as for those working in environments that are not considered "secular", such as Christian ministries and other charities. It also touches our homes. Most Christian homemakers would agree that domestic activities and work share some common characteristics – although not the salaries! This work environment can certainly generate similar stresses and strains.

You probably find yourself somewhere in that wide-ranging list. I hope so, because I'm convinced that the question in the title is one that we all need to answer on a very regular basis. Indeed, I find it difficult to imagine either a time or a context in which it is not applicable.

What is it designed to achieve? Above all, this book is intended to stimulate thought, prayerful reflection and action. The ideal outcome would be that more Christians bring their faith back into their work. After all, Christianity is a set of beliefs that should affect our behavior. It's just possible that you have not thought about work in the way it is considered here, and therefore you may never have felt the full force of biblical teaching on your own behavior. My prayer is, therefore, that this book will lead us all as Christian readers to have a more integrated approach to our whole lives – including our work. The Bible knows no other approach! After all, God calls us to serve and glorify him in every part of our being and in every area of our lives.

Style and sources The book is based on the Bible and focuses on applying its principles. In the pages that follow we are more concerned about the fundamentals of Christian living in the work environment than about techniques for witnessing. There are some excellent complementary books on that subject to which I on occasion refer the reader. Throughout, the book addresses difficult situations in work life and examines their consequences for Christians. The approach is an honest one – not merely offering a theology of work that does not relate to where Christians have to live every day. This is not a technical book, nor is it presented in theological language. It's written in an accessible style, with regular breaks for personal reflection and challenge. Illustrations, case studies, life examples and personal incidents are extensively used – many of them from my own experience, suitably disguised where necessary.

For almost all of my Christian life, since my days as a student, I have been an avid reader of Christian literature. Many Christian writers have made a profound contribution to my life, and it is inevitable that I have reflected some of their thinking here. Where possible, these writers are acknowledged – either in the text or in the short list of further reading at the end of each chapter. In other instances, I have illustrated various points using relevant quotations from some standard sources.[i]

Structure The various issues we will explore in order to answer our core question are divided into four related parts. In Part One, Guiding Principles for Our Work, Chapter 1 introduces the overarching question of the book, looks at the artificial separation of faith and work, and sets out the relationships with work that God presumes for his people. Chapter 2 then explains what it is that is special to God about our individual work and asks whether God is in our attitudes to it. Part Two, Keeping a Perspective on Our Work, deals with that important topic in Chapter 3, exploring the paradoxes surrounding work and outlining the Christian way of making sense of the world of work. Part Three, Learning through the Practice of Our Work, includes Chapters 4 to 8. These five chapters cover issues ranging from being aware of dangers at work; recognizing that work generates conflict with our colleagues and our owner; meeting the challenges of discipleship at work; dealing with the moral dilemmas posed in many work environments; and meeting crises in our personal experiences of work. Part Four, Progressing in Our Work with God, comprises Chapters 9 and 10. Chapter 9 considers how we need to work in line with God's plan, while Chapter 10 draws out our response to the core question as we weigh our work in the correct set of balances.

Acknowledgments So many people have wittingly or unwittingly provided the raw material for this book throughout my working life. I am grateful to them all – although I did not always feel that way when I worked with some of them! My gratitude extends to many others who read and helpfully commented on *Whose Life Is It Anyway?* and encouraged me to write further on such practical topics. These people, along with other business colleagues, were among those who were kind enough to endorse that book. I am once more much indebted to my personal assistant, Irene Hood, for help with this and many similar projects over the past decade and more. Mark Finnie and his whole team at Authentic have been very professional and encouraging throughout the whole process of tuning my mind, spirit and laptop to the realm of Christian writing. They deserve my sincere and unreserved thanks for that. Peter Little deserves special mention for his outstanding work on the design and production of these books. Finally I am, once again, most grateful for the sterling and insightful contribution of my truly gifted editor, Tara Smith.

Neil Hood
October 2002

[1] These quotations have come from a wide range of reference works, including: *Gathered Gold*, compiled by John Blanchard (Darlington: Evangelical Press, 1984); *Sifted Silver,* compiled by John Blanchard (Darlington: Evangelical Press, 1984); Edythe Draper, *Quotations for the Christian World* (Wheaton, IL: Tyndale, 1992); F.B. Proctor, *Treasury of Quotations on Religious Subjects* (Grand Rapids MI: Kregel Publications, 1977); *5000 Quotations for Teachers and Preachers*, compiled by Robert Backhouse (Eastbourne: Kingsway Publications, 1994).

Professor Neil Hood
Biographical Note

Neil Hood, CBE, FRSE, juggles a busy life as an international business strategist, university professor, Christian conference speaker, prolific author on international business and economic development, family man and church elder. He is Professor of Business Policy at the University of Strathclyde, Glasgow, UK, and a director of, or advisor to, a number of major companies, including Scottish Power plc, Xansa plc, British Polythene Industries plc and Reg Vardy plc. He has advised many governments on economic matters, is Deputy Chairman of Scottish Enterprise, and Chairman of Scottish Equity Partners Ltd. In 2000 he was honoured by Queen Elizabeth for services to business and economic development. His life plan to dedicate his time and skills to Christian ministries is reflected in his chairmanship of Send the Light Ltd., in his involvement with Christian ministries such as Scripture Union and Blythswood Care, and in his busy preaching and teaching schedule. He and his wife, Anna, have two children, Annette (married to Alan) and Cameron (married to Ann), and two grandchildren, Emily and Isla. Neil is not too busy, however, to grow orchids, cheer on the Scottish rugby team, play with his grandchildren ... or pray that *Whose Work is it Anyway?* will encourage you to revisit God's involvement in your work.

PART ONE

GUIDING PRINCIPLES FOR OUR WORK

1
Work, the Bible and You

"Do not work for food that spoils, but for food that endures to eternal life, which the Son of Man will give you. On him God the Father has placed his seal of approval." (Jn. 6:27)

Outline   This chapter introduces the book and our core question. It also explores some of the challenges that face Christians in the work environment and outlines principles that are foundational for understanding the biblical view of work. The chapter asks three questions and sounds a note of warning.

Whose work is it anyway?: An introduction
This, the central question, is set in the context of our lives. Then we consider a series of very different Christian responses to the relationship between work and faith.

How do I relate to the secular view of work?
A comparison between the world's view of work and the Christian's view reveals fundamental differences. This section confronts the Christian's temptation to keep work and faith separate.

What kind of relationship with work does the Bible presume?
This section sets out six of the foundational biblical principles concerning work.

A warning and a challenge
The warning concerns how receptive our world is likely to be to our practicing the Christian way at work. The chapter concludes by posing some searching personal questions about the application of these principles.

Whose work is it anyway?: An introduction For many of us, this is an awkward, difficult and demanding question. Perhaps it's one you would prefer not to answer. When I first thought about this book, I wasn't sure I wanted to answer this question either. I suppose I've known the Christian answer to this question for years, but I have feared the implications of living it out. Being a follower of Jesus Christ is one thing, but taking him into each and every work situation is quite another. And, even then, introducing him there would not in itself be enough. God's call is to behave as Jesus would have behaved. I know that I am not alone in being profoundly troubled by this challenge.

Our co-workers may or may not have strong belief systems or faith of any kind

To some degree, the nature of the challenge lies in the complexity and diversity of our work environments. The people we work with are invariably very different and have a variety of personalities and needs. They range from the consistently friendly and open to the permanently restless and negative. Their lives mirror both triumph and tragedy. Our co-workers may or may not have strong belief systems or faith of any kind. Their interests and aspirations are all different, as are their attitudes to work, interpersonal skills, their ability to communicate and listen and so on. All of these differences emerge before we even consider what they think of our faith and what behavior they expect from us when we testify to being Christians. But the differences do not even stop there. When working with people we face many stresses and strains in relationships, personality clashes and different reactions to work pressures. Handling change at work, especially when it has a negative effect on us personally, is another difficult issue. And what about having to make tough decisions about people in areas such as promotion, discipline, sickness and lay offs? Daily work brings us a constant stream of moral choices, both large and small. The way we make these choices adds up to our Christian behavior.

But diversity is only one of the many dimensions of the challenge. We also have to consider our attitude to work and the different motivations that drive us. Money, fulfillment, self-esteem, status, striving for a better society and necessity are but a few of the motivating factors that appear in surveys on this subject. Meanwhile, for an increasing number of people, happiness and work are apparently not closely related – while stress and work evidently are. Equally, long working hours appear to be less connected to more productive work than they are to sickness and fatigue. Christians are not exempt from these pressures – and they affect our behavior in the workplace.

This is only a small sample of the myriad of issues that we typically face on a daily basis. Already we are tempted to say that it is too difficult to link being a Christian with the secular world of work – it would be better to keep these two worlds apart. For many of us, giving in to that temptation is a real danger. But we cannot be truly Christian if we try to keep living and working apart, by whatever means. Difficult though it is, it is to this that God has called us.

But we cannot be truly Christian if we try to keep living and working apart, by whatever means

So that you can understand my perspective and know that I relate closely to, and feel passionately about, this subject, let me share how work affects my life. But first, I acknowledge my own lifelong struggle to keep a balance between home, family, church and work. I have never found this easy and I encourage you to remember this as you read on. Because of the diversity of my interests in business, academic and public life, no two work days are the same for me. I have constantly to adjust to different places, people and environments. Few of them are in any way receptive to Christian faith. Some are openly hostile and marked by their cynicism. The work I do is invariably with strong-willed, successful and highly focused people. Sometimes I am managing them directly; in other contexts I advise them. I travel a lot and work long and irregular hours. Problems and challenges abound. And a lot of my life is lived in the public eye. My work is very diverse. For example, I might be simultaneously helping to grow a business and hire senior people, while working with a large program of lay offs in another company and feeling the real pain of such decisions. Meanwhile I might be mentoring someone through a business or personal crisis, or both. On other days I will be working on a radical change program in an organization, knowing that this will have a profound impact on the lives of many people. As part of my responsibility for the governance of companies, I might be trying to resolve complex ethical problems in different cultures or make commercially risky decisions in an informed way. I work a lot, and I constantly face the

TABLE 1.1
Responses to "Whose work is it anyway?"
"I have no idea! But the last person I would want to associate with this job I hate is God – if that's what you are implying. Do you know anything about the real world?"
"This is not a valid question. I only work for my employer, and that's that. If I want to know for whom I work, I just look at my monthly bank statement. Of course I'm a Christian – but that's another dimension of my life."
"I know the answer to this question. The Bible shows me that my work belongs to God, but I don't have any idea how that might make a difference in what I actually do every day. The whole issue is a mystery to me."
"Good question – but I can't see how biblical principles on work derived from a totally different environment can have anything to say about my work. The Bible is just not good on this kind of stuff."
"I've been a Christian for years and have genuinely opened up all of my life to God – but I've never been asked this question before. I'm not sure that I can handle the answer, especially if it means changing my behavior."
"The thought of really bringing God into my work situation scares me. My attempts at Christian witness there have been rebuffed for years and I'm struggling as it is. I just can't take this any further."
"I have a seriously important and senior job, you know. Yes, I'm a Christian – but I'm also my own man. The pastor has touched on some of these issues, but I filed them all in my in-basket. After all, what does he know about business and professional life? And anyway, I didn't get where I am by being Christ-like."
"Depends what you mean. There are times when I'm very Christian at work – I'm great with illness and family problems. But this is a rough industry; hard decisions need hard hearts, you know. I was never a fan of soft management skills. Tough, but fair, that's me."
"I did know that God had a plan for my life and my career, but I didn't know that it extended into my behavior at work. It's something that I'm not always proud of. This blows my mind. Where do I go from here?"

reality that God can be crowded out of my life. He sometimes is. Yet I am clear that he wants me where I am and that he has a specific expectation of me to live for him in all circumstances. Is it always comfortable? No. Do I always represent God well? No. Do I sometimes hanker for a simpler, less pressure-filled life? Yes – even if only momentarily. Those who know me best smile at this prospect. But there are real tensions for all of us in our relationships with work, and I readily acknowledge them in my life. That is why I have written this book.

One of the latent and universal, yet unresolved, areas of tension between the old creature and the new creature in Christ lies right here. Is it my employer's work? Or is it God's? In what sense can it be both? Not only is the question unresolved – it's often not even discussed or confronted in Christian teaching. Why? It's probably because it falls into that "very difficult" area. Few Christians are confident that the Bible has much to say about work-life problems in the twenty-first century. Over the years I have had many conversations with Christians on this and related subjects. Table 1.1, on p.6, sets out some of the views I have heard expressed. You might relate to some of them. Indeed, I might be describing you. Others you might think are not very "Christian" – and therein lies part of the tension.

☑ **ACTION:** Do any of these comments describe your attitude to work, now or at some time in the past? Try to write down a short description of how your faith relates to your work as you begin to read this book. We will revisit these views later.

Do any of the responses in Table 1.1 sound familiar? At least some of them probably do. These responses suggest confusion, anxiety, a wide variety of interpretations of appropriate Christian behavior, a perceived gap between faith and work and so on. They should not surprise us; nor should we judge. These views do, however, highlight some of the potential danger areas in the Christian's relationship with work. These dangers include partitioning our lives, losing our sense of calling and being shaped by the world's behavior. The reality is that, for some Christians, the duty to self is the greatest of the commandments. It's not just busy people under pressure who face these hazards. We all do. Sherman and Hendricks say that "faith and work is a raw, open nerve for many Christians".¹ While the goal of the material that follows is to heal this wound, cleaning and dressing a wound can be painful – and some aspects of this topic are difficult to confront. In all of this, however, we have the power and strength of the great physician himself.

How do I relate to the secular view of work?

Because a person's attitudes to work and experiences of work are very personal, generalization is difficult. But the prevailing "spirit of the age" surrounding work has created a worldview with common features in most developed countries. Whether we like it or not, this is the air we breathe. This view might even be implicit in the contract you hold with your employer. He hired you because he thought that everybody has this kind of philosophy of life. This worldview includes the beliefs that success means attaining both wealth and status, and that this success is derived from achievements at work. How many times have you heard, "I've made it!" after a promotion? Driven by these imperatives, there is much evidence of the spirit of expediency. "To succeed is tough, therefore I will do whatever it takes to achieve it." This type of statement is often made palatable by the vague qualification of "within limits" – to suggest a moderated and tolerable type of behavior. Those who hold to this view believe that the purpose of work is seen as self-fulfillment – one by-product of which can be that a career becomes an idol. Furthermore, I compare my idol with yours. So we have a futures market in false gods. We are all worshipping them and eagerly anticipating their promises. As has been said, "Too many Christians worship their work, work at their play and play at their worship". Sadly, this is all too often true. Others try to disguise this idolatry and their motivations with statements such as, "This is all for the family"; "I work to live, not live to work"; "I will know when I have enough money/ success/status, and then take life easy" and so on. God is nowhere to be seen in any of these features of the secular view of work – not least because each person designs his own god. We will pause here as we approach a serious hazard.

☑ **ACTION:** Lots of Christians are tempted to try to weave God into such secular perspectives on work by attempting to spiritualize their own behavior. Ask yourself whether you are doing this; and think hard about the consequences. How would you describe in a few words how work fits into your life?

You probably recognize at least some of the above features as representing the world of work. Is the world of Christian faith to be regarded as a separate and very different world? It is tempting, and sometimes convenient, to think this way. Three sets of behavior can flow from this type of compartmentalized thinking, as illustrated by the following simple picture of a house with two rooms.

1. The rooms of faith and of work are never simultaneously occupied. There is a connecting door and we simply walk from one to the other as required. The two rooms are in the same house, but the activities that take place in each are largely separate. This is the way we like it. It keeps life simple.

2. We demonize the work room as somewhere we go under a set of compulsions such as earning a living, supporting our lifestyle, complying with social norms and so on. We are there reluctantly, and somehow it is less important than what happens in the faith room. There is more threat there than there is opportunity. Indeed, we might even feel rather guilty about being at work too often or even being there at all. Being in the faith room is a much higher calling.

3. We see the faith room as a good place to be. Life there, on the whole, is comfortable. But our tendency is to discount the value of faith – either because it appears too demanding or because it seems not entirely applicable to the work room. This attitude is often a long-term consequence of being polluted by the atmosphere that surrounds us at work. Faith ultimately suffers. Indeed, we end up only needing the work room to live in, and we leave the faith room for others to occupy. The end product of this is spiritual emptiness.

Without overanalyzing the metaphor, think about where you stand in this picture. Lots of us are most comfortable with a lifestyle of daily commuting between the faith and work rooms. You might tend towards behaving in one of these ways rather than another. An honest appraisal of our experience might suggest, however, that we often display all three types of behavior. In so doing we reveal how we really relate to the secular world of work.

What kind of relationship with work does the Bible presume?

The theme text for this chapter from John 6 implicitly raises this question. Do Jesus' words here infer that our daily work is always to be regarded as inferior? Or does he mean that we should stop working for a living? Or is it that our daily work contributes nothing to what God is doing in the world? By looking at what Jesus says in the context of the Bible as a whole, we can see that he implies none of these things. Rather, he is addressing here the specific problem of attitudes to work. His audience seemed to be solely interested in material and physical satisfaction. Apparently they could not lift their minds above this. Jesus' words were cautionary to his audience then, and they are even more so now. Jesus Christ directed this teaching to bring a fresh focus to their living by pointing them towards himself. And Jesus clearly explains this guidance, "on him the Father has set his seal of approval". This sign of authenticity is vital to us. Only Christ can satisfy eternal hunger; only he can put our lives into perspective and guide us to know the answer to "Whose work is it anyway?".

Only Christ can satisfy eternal hunger

The question before us, "What kind of relationship with work does the Bible presume?", will recur throughout the book in many different contexts. At this stage we need to establish and understand some of the basic biblical principles concerning work. I have selected six of these principles, all of which are interrelated. We will then build on these in subsequent chapters. As you think about these principles and begin to relate them to your work, recall the words of James Moffat. "Great as is the power of God, he cannot work in a vacuum or with empty minds or with hearts filled with prejudice." This subject will engage our minds and our hearts in a very practical way.

God as a worker

From the first pages in the Bible, the subject of work confronts us. For example, the creation record refers several times to God engaging in work and to his satisfaction with what he had made. "God saw all that he had made, and it was very good."[2] This activity was evidently something that, having been completed, led to his being refreshed and rested. We see this in Exodus, "On the seventh day he rested, and was refreshed".[3] Thus, even in these early references, we see traces of both God's attitudes to work and his behavior in it. But it does not stop there. God starts with creation and moves on to the work of providence, judgment and redemption. God's work is creative, orderly and constructive. In all of this, God enjoys perfect job satisfaction (something we rarely have). Although unique, the work of God remains a model for human work – in spite of the fact that the connection between the work we do and its contribution to God's work is not always obvious.

God and human beings as co-workers The principle of being co-workers with God is also established early in the Bible and consistently reinforced throughout. God planted a garden and charged humankind to cultivate and protect it.[4] Human and divine co-operation abounds as people become partners with God. "Unless the LORD builds the house, its builders labor in vain".[5] In this context, the attitude of the worker towards God is one of dependence, service and worship. The result of that attitude is evident in passages such as "May the favor of the Lord our God rest upon us; establish the work of our hands for us – yes, establish the work of our hands".[6] There is little doubt that the Bible sees our work, provided it is work in which God can be honored, as being done in co-operation with him. But this collaboration has other consequences as well. It implies that we seek to apply as much of God's model of work as possible. In this relationship we are the junior partners, and we are learning from our Master. What

God planted a garden and charged humankind to cultivate and protect it

implications, for example, does this have for seeking to maintain harmonious relationships at work? For our work being characterized by order and creativity? For us being satisfied within it? It is possible to conclude (and sometimes we do so too readily) that, because of sin, none of our work completely fulfills God's intentions. In later chapters we will look in more depth at just how practical and possible all this is.

Work as a calling The biblical sense of Christian "calling" is first and foremost that we are called to belong to Jesus Christ. It's a calling to belong to and imitate Christ in all dimensions of life – including where we work. "That's just fine", you might say, "I've no problem with this in principle." But it doesn't just stop there – there's much more detail to come. As John White observes, "It is one thing to know how God thinks, it is quite another to want what he wants". Paul, in his letter to the Corinthians, says that "Each one should remain in the situation which he was in when God called him".[7] You might well ask what this can possibly mean in today's geographically and socially mobile society. Paul was illustrating the point that the particular calling of God reaches into every part of our lives. In this context the focus was on the domestic, cultural, social and occupational aspects of their lives. There was no hiding place for them, any more than there is for us in this matter. It's possible that you and I do not always like what God has called us to do. We would prefer a different job, in another place or in a distant culture. Such a spirit of discontent can blind us from ever seeing our current work as a calling. It is worth noting that Jesus took time out to answer questions from tax collectors and soldiers who were asking how they should display his moral and spiritual values in their occupations now that they had come to follow him.[8] He told the former to be honest in their tax collection, and he told the latter not to extort money or falsely accuse people and to be content with their pay. Pretty detailed stuff!

Work as stewardship It is tempting, when considering the important biblical principle that work is intended for self-fulfillment, to forget that it is also part of our stewardship of God's resources vested in us. In terms of self-fulfillment, the instruction "Be fruitful and increase in number; fill the earth and subdue it"[9] does point to part of God's purpose for our lives. Yet, for many people, the concept of self-fulfillment through the particular work they do is very difficult. Monotony, risk, persecution and the pressing necessity to earn money might be among the many reasons for this. Viewing work as stewardship can be no less challenging for similar reasons. Christians hold three things in stewardship, and they each have a work dimension. First, we have natural talents from birth – the parts of our personalities, skills and aptitudes that mark the similarities and differences between us. These natural talents usually shape our choice of work. Second, we have the truth of the gospel, the indwelling Spirit and the gifts received from God. We did not know about these when we were born, but we were told about them and

we have the truth of the gospel, the indwelling Spirit and the gifts received from God

they have affected our lives. The Bible assumes that these are indelibly engraved in our hearts. Finally, we hold in stewardship the possessions acquired during our lifetimes – these we have generally accumulated by applying our skills and experience to work. The foundational biblical principle is that all three categories of resources belong to the Lord. The first two we take to work every day, whether we use them there or not, although there is no doubt that Jesus expects us to apply these to our daily work. See, for example, the parable of the talents in Matthew's gospel.[10] The worker is a steward who serves his master, and the master in turn gives the opportunity to work and sets the time frame. The worker has a choice as to how to deploy the resources given to him and must exercise moral responsibility in their use. The master judges on the basis of service and the reward is his approval. It's interesting to note that there are no financial rewards here. Approval in and of itself is enough for these workers – very unlike the expectations of reward in our world. Rather troubling, isn't it?

Work as service

Closely linked to both calling and stewardship is the principle that work is not only for self-fulfillment but also for the benefit of the community. In the great Philippian passage on imitating Christ's humility, Paul writes, "Each of you should look not only to your own interests, but also to the interests of others".[11]

In effect, where we might place an either/or between service to God and the community, the Bible assumes that we think of our work as both. John Stott takes this further. "Certainly the Bible regards work as a community project, undertaken by the community for the community. All work needs to be seen as being, at least to some degree, public service."[12] This idea is probably not foremost in our minds. The ethic of service is more evident, perhaps, in caring professions, although I regularly hear Christians who work in these jobs disagree because of the pressures under which they function. Many types of work that we engage in, and many of the attitudes that we take to work, seem to be quite distant from this ideal. Moreover, some of the work decisions that we have to make bring out the tensions between public and private interests. For example, sometimes people lose their jobs for the good of the whole organization, it can be difficult to balance safety at work with practical operations, and so on. But

All work needs to be seen as being, at least to some degree, public service

there is a wider social aspect of this service, namely that of viewing our work as enabling us to help others in need. For example, in his teaching on living as children of light, Paul observes, "He who has been stealing must steal no longer, but must work, doing something useful with his own hands, that he may have something to share with those in need".[13] We need to be forcefully reminded of this in a society in which many Christian people see their incomes as being primarily (or solely) to sustain a lifestyle to which they aspire. The needs of others rarely come into their reckoning.

Work as bringing glory to God

This is perhaps the most challenging principle of all, because it is all-embracing. I can see some of my work doing this, but not all of it, and not all of the time. It can be good work by earthly standards, my way of doing it can be laudable and my behavior exemplary – but it still may not bring glory to God. The "gap" may be in my motives, in my attitudes, or even in my testimony when no one around me knows who my real Master is. "Bringing glory" implies that God's purposes are revealed and fulfilled. "So whether you eat or drink or whatever you do, do it all for the glory of God."[14]

"So whether you eat or drink or whatever you do, do it all for the glory of God."

This principle by its very nature infers an act of worship in our work. And, for many of us, work does not often feel like something that can be considered worshipful. I'm convinced, however, that God does not want to keep us in the dark about how we can bring him glory in our work. Faithfully applying the six principles set out here will bring God glory. Our work can be our witness, but we usually need to use both actions and words. Augustine was right when he said, "What I live by, I impart".

A warning and a challenge

The German theologian Christoph Ernst Luthhardt was correct in observing that "the view we entertain of God will determine our view of the world". As we have reflected on these principles regarding work, we are all aware that the world around us is not neutral as to how we try to apply them. Let me suggest that God is not neutral either. These principles are part of his instruction to us that we ignore at our peril. Know your God, know your world is a sound principle. In general, the world around us is hostile to faith. John expresses it in these terms, "For everything in the world – the cravings of sinful man, the lust of his eyes and the boasting of what he has and does – comes not from the Father but from the world. The world and its desires pass away, but the man who does the will of God lives forever".[15] Jim Packer translates the essence of this verse by describing "everything" as encompassing the pleasure, profit, power and promotion motives. Christians share some of these motives; it would be dishonest to deny that. But verse 17 confronts us with the simple truth that the world and its value systems have a limited life. We will not find the true answer to our question by pursuing them. We will develop this important issue further in Chapter 5.

I'll let C.S. Lewis have the last word: "There is no neutral ground in the universe: every square inch, every split second is claimed by God and counter claimed by Satan". That's the battle we should expect to wage as we ask God to give us a fresh perspective on our personal world of work.

Challenge No1

Take the opportunity here to pause, think and pray. Take each of these six principles and test them against your present practice at work. This might lead you to ask the following types of questions:

1 Is God's model of work in any way reflected in my behavior at work and in my attitude to work?

2 Am I conscious of God as a co-worker?

3 To what extent do I regard my present work as God's calling for me?

4 Do I take all of God's resources that I have in stewardship to my work? How can I make preparations to do this each day?

5 What sense do I have of serving God and the community in my work? And where does it show?

6 In what way does my behavior at work bring glory to God?

Further reading

Field, David, *The Bible and Christian Living* (London: Scripture Union, 1987).

Stott, John, *The Contemporary Christian* (Leicester: IVP, 1992).

Triton, A.N., *Whose World?* (London: IVP, 1970).

Yancey, Philip, *Reaching for the Invisible God* (Grand Rapids: Zondervan, 2000).

Endnotes

1 Doug Sherman and William Hendricks, *Your Work Matters to God* (Colorado Springs: NavPress, 1987).

2 Gen. 1:31.

3 Ex. 31:17 (RSV).

4 Gen. 2:15.

5 Ps. 127:1.

6 Ps. 90:17.

7 1 Cor. 7:20.

8 Lk. 3:12-14.

9 Gen. 1:28.

10 Mt. 25:14-30.

11 Phil. 2:4.

12 John Stott, *Issues Facing Christians Today* (London: Marshall Pickering, rev. edn, 1999).

13 Eph. 4:28.

14 1 Cor. 10:31.

15 1 Jn. 2:16-17.

2
The Importance of Your Work in God's Eyes

"The Word became flesh and lived for a while among us. We have seen his glory, the glory of the one and only, who came from the Father, full of grace and truth." (Jn. 1:14)

Outline   Before we look further at how to make sense of the world of work from a biblical perspective, we need to consider how God sees the work in which we are engaged. Unless we each know how our work matters to God and how it can make a difference for his kingdom, we run the risk of seeing faith at work as an optional extra. This chapter poses two central questions and then takes a brief look at some biblical pictures highlighting the attitudes God desires at work.

What's so special about my work?
We examine the following four elements of Christian character in order to better understand our personal work responsibilities for God: to be a witness; to be shaped by God; to show God's love in action; and to bring him glory.

Is God in my attitudes to work?
This section stresses the vital importance of this question by thinking about some aggressive contemporary attitudes to work that daily surround us.

The attitudes at work that God wants
This final section looks at three of the words that the New Testament uses to describe a Christian: God's temple, God's partner, God's disciple. Some challenging lessons emerge from the attitudes at work that are implicit in these pictures.

What's so special about my work?

We concluded the first chapter with six biblical principles concerning work, but I often find myself one step removed from these principles. In this second foundational chapter we will flesh out these principles personally and practically as we seek to answer our core question, "Whose work is it anyway?". It is very easy to be so caught up in the daily routine – the preoccupation with tasks and deadlines, the need to respond to the pressures and changing demands of work – that we lose any real sense that our work actually matters to God. Christians are wisely advised to start the day with God and reaffirm their sense of purpose and mission. But it is all too easy to overlook that discipline in the hustle and bustle of the day. It is necessary but not sufficient to make us aware that the work that each of us does, as well as how we behave while at work, are of real importance to God. If I can discern God's purposes in my work at all, to what extent can I do this? Work, with all its minutiae, can so dominate each hour of our working day (as well as our time outside of work) that we forget the strategic reason why God has placed us where we are. In fact, many Christians seem quite unaware that there is any strategy at all behind why we do what we do.

"What's special to God about my work?"

There are plenty of people (Christians among them) who will readily bore you for hours with the details of what's special about their work. In doing so, they are really responding to the question, "What is special to me about my work?". On the negative side, this type of conversation betrays traces of self-importance, power, professional status, earning power and so on. More positively, all people need to feel that their work is worthwhile and contributes to both their needs and those of society. Few people dislike talking about their work. We are seeking the answer to a rather different question, however: namely, "What's special to God about my work?". As we shall see, to find the answer to that question we need to understand God's intentions for his disciples. It's highly improbable that the God who called us to follow him does not have a purpose for us in the place where many of us spend two-thirds of our time and up to half of our lives. To deny this purpose would be to presume a very partial calling and a rather spurious form of discipleship. In addition to understanding the nature of discipleship, we need to consider the spirit and attitudes that we bring to our work. John Oxenham's prayer is very challenging in this regard, "Lord, turn the routines of work into celebrations of love". I know that I will never be able to do this until I can answer our core question. So I'm bound to ask what exactly is so special to God about my particular work? What kind of a person does God call me to be in my work situation? The following four dimensions of godly behavior lead us towards an answer.

To be a witness We can only implement Jesus' great commission if we assume that our whole lives are open to his instruction. "Therefore go and make disciples of all nations, baptizing them in the name of the Father and of the Son and of the Holy Spirit, and teaching them to obey everything I have commanded you. And surely I will be with you always."[1] While this passage does not explicitly mention secular work, it is difficult to see how potential disciples could be either reached or taught without engaging with them in work situations. Jesus not only worked as a carpenter himself, but he also went to visit people at their places of work (on their fishing boats, at tax collection offices and so on) and challenged and taught them in terms of living out their faith in these situations.

The great commission includes the instruction to teach the nations "everything" Jesus commanded – and he taught plenty about behavior at work! Jesus' attitude towards our work is a key to its special importance and should destroy any notion we may have of keeping faith and work apart. Our workplace may well be the only place where our colleagues will ever be exposed to Christians. But does that mean that evangelism at work should be our only priority? If this were the case, the actual work that we do would be secondary and of much less significance. We might then regard our work as "only a job" and a means to an end. With such an attitude, we would be unlikely to bring glory to God by our performance and behavior at work. Our work would then fall far short of the standard set in several biblical passages. Ephesians, for example, encourages disciples to "Serve wholeheartedly, as if you were serving the Lord, not men, because you know that the Lord will reward everyone for whatever good he does, whether he is slave or free".[2] Such passages make it very clear that God is looking for excellence in our work, part of which is effective witnessing. It's that combination that's important to him. We are to be living examples that Christianity actually works.

To be shaped by God   It has taken me some time to see how God has used my different work experiences – good and bad – to shape me for his service. It can be difficult to see the bigger picture of how God is shaping us when we have a boss who always takes all the credit or who seems to survive by conflict in all his work relationships, or when we have colleagues who are cynical about our beliefs. These experiences do not always feel like a positive shaping. Yet, for many of us, the places where we have worked and spent so much of our lives have been important for the development of our faith in God. And each of us has been shaped in a different way. On occasion, the more negative the situation is, the more we cling to our faith. God doesn't always change the work, but he does change the worker. Paul attributes much to this divine process in the phrase "we are God's workmanship"[3] – literally, we are his living works of art, with all of the craftsmanship and uniqueness that this picture implies. By a process of "keeping in step with the Spirit",[4] we have come through it. Sadly, not all Christians have persevered through this testing. I know too many young professional Christians who have been shaped more by ambition, money and power than they have by faith. Their relationship with the Lord, once so right, has gone seriously wrong. In contrast, consider how Joseph's ability to provide leadership in Egypt was honed through his experiences of abandonment and slavery. This painful journey finally led to the palace and a unique position of leadership. Similarly, Daniel moved all the way from being a prisoner of war to ruling one third of the kingdom of Babylon. From the outset, his witness at work was awesome. In terms of performance excellence, he and his colleagues were better than their godless peers by a factor of ten.[5] Most of us would be happy with a factor of two. If we allowed God to shape us just as he wants, he would have his special servants in the places where we work. At the moment there might be a void there – a void created by our resistance to his purposes.

> *God doesn't always change the work, but he does change the worker*

This principle of seeing our work in the context of a right relationship with God extends across the widest possible activity spectrum. This book is for all kinds of workers, and so is the Bible. All of us need to know the answer to the question "whose work is it anyway?". In Colossians, for example, slaves (the lowest members of society) were told, "obey your earthly masters in everything; and do it, not only when their eye is on you and to win their favor, but with sincerity of heart and reverence for the Lord. Whatever you do, work at it with all your heart, as working for the Lord, not for men, since you know that you will receive an inheritance from the Lord as a reward".[6] We can scarcely imagine the menial, demeaning and wretched tasks that such slaves did in these times. Yet God himself regarded such work as being done for him. Conversely, the most powerful members of society who had become Christians were called to a very different kind of behavior than they had exhibited in the past. In a world where their slaves had no rights of any kind, in Christ God charged them to "provide your slaves with what is right and fair, because you know that you also have a Master in heaven".[7] What a powerful reflection of the impact of the Spirit on their lives! Christ introduced both parties to a higher dimension to their work, to an overriding set of obligations. Jesus Christ reminded them that he was Lord of their specific work environment. It may be surprising to see the assumption in these passages that God dominates our work. We may try to marginalize him, but that's obviously not his plan. How far short of this plan we all fall!

To show God's love in action Showing God's love is linked to our special role as witnesses but applies more specifically to behavior at work. Now we are in really tough territory. The work behavior of many Christians would not stand up to the scrutiny of their peers, never mind that of the Lord. Some Christians are characterized more by their awkwardness, arrogance, pettiness and bullying tactics than they are by Christ-likeness. The church's greatest handicap is the ungodly lives of those who profess to follow Christ. C.H. Spurgeon once remarked, "If your theology doesn't change your behaviour, it will never change your destiny". When asked what the greatest commandment was, Jesus said, "'Love the Lord your God with all your heart and with all your soul and with all your mind.' ... And the second is like it: 'Love your neighbor as yourself'".[8] This is a challenging mandate – to love God, love others and love ourselves. The practical implications of these words are immense. Loving God involves obedience. How often do we prayerfully analyze our job and work behavior? How often do we ask whether and where the love of God is evident in this behavior? Should our love for God

The work behavior of many Christians would not stand up to the scrutiny of their peers, never mind that of the Lord

not show in the way we treat people, our work methods, our performance, our motives and so on? For example, how is it evident in dealing with a difficult customer in a retail store? In a manager's relationship with an awkward employee? In the life of an exhausted nurse taking care of an ungrateful patient? We might be tempted to ask, "What does love have to do with my work?". The biblical answer is – everything.

But there is a mystery and a reality here. It was within God's power to clone us when he called us. To make us all alike would have somehow been simpler. Yet he has taken us, with all our faults, and through the power of the Spirit God is able to transform us so that we can express his love in our actions – and in our work. That's how a woodworker, a banker, a truck driver, a doctor, a plumber or a teacher does God's work. Part of this love is expressed through relationships at work. But this love is also evident through our other forms of service such as in helping others and caring for our families and for others who are in need. Although William Tyndale wrote these words several centuries ago, they are wholly biblical and contemporary in their application. "There is no work better than another to please God; to pour water, to wash dishes, to be a cobbler, or an apostle, all is one; to wash dishes and to preach is all one, as touching as the deed, to please God."

There is no work better than another to please God

To bring God glory
In this vital matter we face a massive challenge. In our work we are called to lead the people with whom we interact to thank and praise God. For what, you may ask? For what they see of Christ in us; for the Spirit-induced differences in our lives; for our demonstration of the love of Christ; for our practice of faith; for our integrity; for our concern for others and so on. The words "in order that we, who were the first to hope in Christ, might be for the praise of his glory"[9] imply all of that and more. It would be very easy to give up and say that this calling is quite impossible on several counts. "The people I work with neither know nor worship God"; "nobody here thinks like that – if I'm a decent person, they would not know who to thank (if they even thought of thanking anybody)"; "people do notice differences, but only in the usual ways – good or bad, kind or rude and so on – why do they want a reason?"; "this is a dreadful work atmosphere, there's no way that God is getting glory out of

this". All of these responses lead to a single reasonable, if challenging, answer. I will have to both live as a follower of Christ and talk about the person I am following. How else can people make the connection? Christians are called to be more than "good people". This poses problems for some Christians. They rightly contend that it is better to walk than talk. It is necessary, in fact, to both walk and talk. Many of us in the developed world, and especially in Europe, live in post-Christian societies. Large sections of the population have little memory or concept of what it means to follow Christ. Being a Christian is not, in their eyes, materially different from being anything else. People need signposts as to why we behave as we do, and we have to provide them.

The New Testament writers consistently tell us that the glory of God's nature, character, power and purpose are now to be seen in Jesus. As the writer to the Hebrews says, for example, "The Son is the radiance of God's glory and the exact representation of his being, sustaining all things by his powerful word".[10] Our theme text for this chapter is another example. John writes of the voice of God that still speaks through the Bible by the power of the Spirit. Jesus is in us through the Spirit – and, for the moment, warts and all, we are part of that continuing voice. In every sense, the work of "bringing glory" continues, in part, through us. But how will we know if we are bringing glory to God? We may in fact never know in this life. While you can know your cholesterol count, blood pressure or resting heart rate, none of us has a "glory indicator". We are assured, however, that God is pleased with obedience to our calling, and a natural outcome of that obedience is to bring glory to his name. While our task is to manage the inputs to our work, God measures the output.

There is, however, another crucial aspect of bringing God glory. Throughout the Bible, work and worship are closely linked. Indeed, one of the Hebrew words for "work" is on occasion translated as "worship". Mark Greene makes this connection by observing that "work is a seven lettered word".[11] When a Christian works, he is also worshipping. Do you have any sense of that day by day? Wrong attitudes at work and about work are bound to lead to poor quality worship – or to no worship at all. God is thereby "doubly" robbed of

> *Throughout the Bible, work and worship are closely linked*

glory – because we are not leading others to give him glory and because we are not worshipping him ourselves.

The prayer of David, when he was preparing for the temple that his son Solomon was one day to build, set the pattern for all ascriptions of praise in the Bible: "Yours O LORD, is the greatness and the power and the glory and the majesty and the splendor, for everything in heaven and earth is yours. Yours, O LORD, is the kingdom; you are exalted as head over all."[12]

Jesus picked up the essence of this response in the prayer that he taught to his disciples.[13] As William Barclay reminds us, "I cannot say amen [to these words] unless I honestly say, 'Cost what it may, this is my prayer'". Such indeed is the magnitude of the challenge to bring God glory in our life and work.[14]

☑ **ACTION:** We have explored four ways in which we are to contribute to God through our work. Review and assess your own recent job experience in each of these four areas. Pray that you will be able to see this honestly and in a balanced way. We all have a lot to learn about this subject and a long way to go to apply these principles more perfectly. How would you answer the question "What's so special to God about my work?".

Is God in my attitudes to work? The attitudes we bring to our work play a major role in determining what our unique contributions will be. As you went through the exercise above, you probably felt some pain about your current behavior. I know that I have. We explore this further by looking at the "spirit of our age" regarding work. How and where does this spirit affect our work that matters so much to God? What follows is in very sharp contrast to our discussion above. I found the following attitudes as I scanned a number of business magazines that I normally read. I searched the individual and company profiles for some current evidence on prevailing attitudes to work. I did not have to look for long – these role models were brimming over with opinions that seep into the media and training courses all over the world. These people are opinion formers who help to set the context in which many

Christians have to work. Here are ten of their views about themselves or others they admire.

1. "He has always been mindlessly competitive."
2. "This man needs to be a control freak at all times."
3. "He is consumed by ambition."
4. "To succeed, you have to regard everybody else as the enemy."
5. "I regard work as a promotion machine."
6. "He's a person who is amoral in all things – the end always justifies the means."
7. "The secret of my success is, find the money formula first and fast."
8. "The 24-7 work culture suits me; I don't want a family life."
9. "He's adrenalin-fuelled, committed to the max."
10. "A team builder, noted for his delegation and trust – but not too much of either."

You'll notice how assertive and aggressive these statements are. There are some extreme remarks here, and many of them sound very negative. Some levels of ambition and competitiveness might be necessary ingredients of good personal work performance – the kind that brings glory to God. Others, such as the reference to an absence of morals or zero respect for family life, could not be considered Christian. Whether you know many people like these or whether you are a person with similar characteristics may depend on the type of work that you do. You may be at the early stages of a career and such views have so far bypassed you, or you may be in mid-career and all of this sounds like "business as usual". It is not only "the captains of industry", however, who use this language. I have met such driven people in very different walks of life. Many of them would regard being described in some of these ways as a "badge of honor". While they often disdain such pointed language, they show much evidence of these traits. And some of them are Christians.

We saw above that our work is special to God – at least that is what he intended it to be. But whether it is in fact special will depend on our attitudes and behavior. Look again at the ten attitudes above, thinking of it as looking in a mirror where you see both yourself and some parts of your immediate work environment.

> ☑ **ACTION:** Do you display any of these extreme characteristics in your attitudes to work? If you do, think carefully about how that might affect the distinctive contribution from work that God is looking for from you. If you are brave enough, test the opinions of those you work with to see how they perceive you. What will you do to change any ungodly attitudes? If these types of attitudes are evident around you, pray that they will not pollute you.

The attitudes at work that God wants

The One who made us knows our weaknesses – and our potential – and he gave us the Bible as our manual for living. Noting that Christian ethics were not developed either in the cloister or for the cloister, John Stott observed, "... the New Testament context of the Christian life is the noisy, busy, challenging arena of the workplace and the marketplace".[15] What we are doing here, then, is reconnecting something that has too often become disconnected. We can confidently say that it was not the Master's intention to disconnect work and life from faith. To that end, the Bible contains many helpful perspectives on the type of attitudes we need in order to speak for God through our work. In this final section we explore three of them.

God's temple

Paul poses the question, "Don't you know that you yourselves are God's temple and that God's Spirit lives in you?".[16] He goes on to say just how sacred that temple is and that "you are that temple". This is a powerful metaphor. And it is founded on a very high view of men and women. Perhaps, for some of us, this is just too high a view. The expectations built into it might seem beyond our abilities – especially in the work environment. However, the value that Christians have in this world lies in the unique relationship they have with God. That's the working assumption of the Bible. That's what Christ died for. Pressing this picture further, we have to ask ourselves about the activity that goes on in this temple, the extent to which it actually belongs to the living God. Who else lives there? Is this temple of ours a historic monument or a center for worship and witness? Moving into even deeper water, that means that you took the Spirit to that meeting when you behaved mercilessly in berating a junior colleague for a minor offense. The Spirit was there when you lied to the customer about the product problems he has been having. The Spirit witnessed you fudging the expenses claim. The Spirit was there, waiting,

THE IMPORTANCE OF YOUR WORK IN GOD'S EYES

when you had an opportunity to witness but remembered that you never mix faith and work as a matter of principle. If this makes you weep, weep on. Sometimes this is the sad fact of Christian life at work. The issue is not whether I can live like Christ, but whether I can let Christ live in me. My body is the container – is the Spirit evidently in it?

The issue is not whether I can live like Christ, but whether I can let Christ live in me

God's partners The idea of partnership and sharing is integral to Christian life. The very idea of a partnership is rooted in the purely business and commercial sense of the term. As such, it is very relevant to our study of work. No partnership works unless there is sufficient common purpose between the parties; they have to have good reason for being in that relationship; and the reason has to be durable through good and bad times. Partnerships rarely survive for long if one of them is "sleeping", or taking no active part in the relationship. Is "partner with Christ" listed on your physical or mental biodata? Do you have a sense of doing (or not doing) your share of God's work? Without exception, all Christians are named as partners in the grace of God. Paul built on this idea when he thanked God for "partnership in the gospel from the first day until now, being confident of this, that he who began a good work in you will carry it on to completion until the day of Christ Jesus".[17] It is indeed encouraging to find that the Bible recognizes our need for ongoing help to deliver on this role. While a partnership needs strength, it also requires the right spirit. It simply cannot be made to function if I have to be reluctantly dragged into taking the Lord into my working life. You can assume that God has work that he wants you to do together where you work; but in you he may not always have a willing partner.

God's disciples The Christian is characteristically a learner. This must be his lifelong aim – based on an attitude of humility that wants to know more about the person he has pledged to follow. For most of us, work can be a difficult environment – and one in which we all make mistakes. The first rule for every learner is to admit that others may be right and he may be wrong. Unplanned words, unforeseen situations, unhelpful colleagues are only some of the things that can induce behavior in us that is far from Christ-like. We need to remember that what we are learning about is the greatness and all-sufficiency of God in all of life's challenges. Other people need (and some want) to learn that from us. Many people simply don't read the Bible. In our working lives, we do not always hear it in the words expressed to Philip, "Sir, we would like to see Jesus".[18] These truth-seeking Greek travelers exhibited a hunger for God that our peers do not always have. The "request" is often silent; the office mood indifferent; the questioning cynical and sneering; the words taunting. But people do look for the evidence of both our following and our learning. What do they see? If they were taking notes, how would their "diary of a Christian" actually read?

Challenge No 2

This chapter covers some rather personal material about God's expectations of, and our attitudes to, our work. Take time now to spend a few minutes in prayerful reflection about the following:

1 Determine what you think is special to God about your present role at work. It is essential to consider this now, so that the material in the following chapters will be challenging and life-changing.

2 Over recent years, has your work had more impact on you than God has? Or have you felt that God has worked with you to make it possible for you to handle the different attitudes in your work environment?

3 How do you relate to the idea of your current work as "worship"? Think of comparisons with how you prepare for and engage in worship, its impact upon you, your attitude while worshipping, how focused you are and so on.

4 How could you bring more glory to God through your work? Or what has to change in order for you to start to bring him any glory?

5 As you reflect on the pictures of a temple, of partners and of disciples that we looked at in the last section, decide which has the most relevance for how you relate to your work.

6 One conclusion that a Christian could draw from this chapter is, "I work for God". Are you able to say that?

Further reading

Dunn, Jim, *Lifewise Guide to Work* (Eastbourne: Kingsway Publications, 2000).

Green, Michael, and Alister McGrath, *How Shall We Reach Them?* (Milton Keynes: Nelson Word, 1994).

Tippett, Sammy, *The Prayer Factor* (Amersham: Scripture Press Foundation, 1989).

Westcott, David, *Work Well: Live Well: Rediscovering a Biblical View of Work* (London: Marshall Pickering, 1996).

Endnotes

1 Mt. 28:18-20.

2 Eph. 6:7-8.

3 Eph. 2:10.

4 Gal. 5:25.

5 Dan. 1:20.

6 Col. 3:22-24.

7 Col. 4:1.

8 Mt. 22:37, 39.

9 Eph. 1:12.

10 Heb. 1:3.

11 Mark Greene, *Thank God It's Monday: Ministry in the Workplace* (London: Scripture Union, 1994), p. 36.

12 1 Chr. 29:11.

13 Mt. 6:9-13.

14 You might like to pursue this further by reading William Barclay, *The Plain Man Looks at the Lord's Prayer* (London: Collins, 1964).

15 John Stott, *The Incomparable Christ* (Leicester: IVP, 2001), pp. 96-97.

16 1 Cor. 3:16.

17 Phil. 1:5-6.

18 Jn. 12:21.

PART TWO

KEEPING A PERSPECTIVE ON OUR WORK

3
Making Sense of the World of Work

"But in your hearts set apart Christ as Lord."
(1 Pet. 3:15)

Outline   We now move from foundational principles about work to some of the pressing issues that confront us as we try to orient ourselves in our work environment. Chief among these concerns is confusion about the world of work – where work is heading and how we fit into it. All of the following issues can and do disturb Christians. It is essential to understand work from a Christian perspective. In this chapter we address three questions and end with a series of biblical lessons about "making sense while standing still".

What paradoxes do we find in work?
This section examines five areas of inconsistency, including work itself, time, age, stress and identity.

What's happening to work?
This section briefly reviews some of the major trends affecting work and current issues that often make work "feel different" for Christians. Included in this list are risk and uncertainty, change, individualism, performance, morality and pollution.

Is there a Christian way of making sense of work?
Convinced that the answer to this question is "yes", we explore here the need for a fresh perspective, clear vision and a renewed spirit – each of which can only come from the Lord.

Making sense while being still
Based on three different cases in which people were asked to be still to be delivered, instructed and restored, we explore the relevance of all three to our relationship with work.

What paradoxes do we find in work? This chapter builds upon the first two, which set out some of the great biblical principles concerning work and rooted these in how we contribute to God's kingdom through our work. This chapter focuses not so much on a comprehensive review of the many ways work is changing as it does on asking how Christians might interpret and respond to such changes. Whatever the context (and each one varies considerably), can we make (Christian) sense of work? We would probably all agree that at times this is really difficult. Yet without such an understanding it is unlikely that we will be effective Christians at work through the various twists and turns of career, circumstances, employment opportunities, family responsibilities, health and so on. Christians take comfort from the fact that "Jesus Christ is the same yesterday and today and forever"[1] and cling to such biblical constants in times of change. But we can too easily forget these assurances in the midst of difficult situations. It is tempting to respond to the many complexities of the work environment by saying that we simply cannot make any sense of them. But that's scarcely good enough. God's purpose is not best served by our wandering in the dark. Part of the confusion surrounding the world of work lies in the many paradoxes associated with it. As we consider five of these paradoxes below, we will see that each one has Christian consequences.

Work The first issue about which it is easy to make self-contradictory statements is work itself. Work is something we all need to do, yet most of us seem to have either too much or too little of it; work is either too exhausting or not challenging enough; work can generate excessive rewards or none at all. For some, work is characterized by chronic busyness, while for others its most striking feature is crushing boredom. Some people seem incapable of anything other than total commitment to their work, while others have a casual relationship with it and seem to perpetually live at the edge of the job market. Some members of our society are almost too qualified for the jobs that are available, while others do not have enough skills. There are Christians in all of these different categories, and some face such paradoxes on a daily basis. The type of work available to us also varies, and not always in the ways we want. In countries such as the United Kingdom, the United States and France, only between 50 and 60 per cent of

Work is something we all need to do, yet most of us seem to have either too much or too little of it

workers are in full-time employment; with many others of working age employed part-time, in contract employment or self-employed. Work is associated with status and standing, and its absence with the opposite. Charles Handy expresses this well. "We seem to have made work a god and then made it difficult for many to worship".[2]

Time We think that we should have more time, yet we appear to have less. In spite of the fact that people now generally live longer and have higher levels of efficiency and more leisure, we never seem to have enough time. In order to accommodate other societal changes, organizations tend to offer more time flexibility in work contracts. Meanwhile, many people feel overworked – in part because they need more money and in part because the organizations that employ them want to operate with fewer people. Lots of people simply choose to have little time in order to maximize the money they earn or (more unusually), vice versa. This battle with time has several consequences for the Christian. In some jobs, it's clear that both success and survival are on a collision course with marriage and parenthood as God designed them. Neither do many of us have the time to form relationships with people as "salt and light". The societies in which many of us live operate seven days a week to support the high service levels that we expect, to accommodate demands for leisure and so on. Christian service suffers and the church is the poorer because some of its best resources are lost to this lack of time. In such situations (and many of us are in them), something has to change. We will return to this issue later in the book.

The societies in which many of us live operate seven days a week to support the high service levels that we expect

Age There are also many paradoxes with regard to age and work, and particularly concerning skill and experience. While many organizations trumpet that their real asset is people, they seem content to lose the skills and experience of relatively young people through early retirement. Increased life expectancy, together with the growing costs of financing retirement and low population growth, are beginning to contribute to a reversal of that trend in some countries, which will produce an older cadre of workers. Some of these workers will have a portfolio of different activities, part paid and part voluntary. Churches that have long benefited from healthy early retirees may no longer do so. Another age paradox for older Christians is much (apparent) leisure, but no spare time. I meet many highly skilled Christians who cannot think what they could possibly do with their skills for God in their retirement. So they just travel a lot. There are many others who have much to offer and have a different answer to "Whose work is it anyway?". They may not all agree with Jonathan Swift's remark "that no wise man ever wished to be younger". But their work continues in this spirit, "And whatever you do, whether in word or deed, do it all in the name of the Lord Jesus, giving thanks to God the Father through him".[3] This is good advice for all ages, all times and all cultures.

Stress The issue of stress can also be full of paradox for Christians. "I am convinced that I am in the job God wants me to do. But why is it so very stressful? And why is it getting worse?" There are usually several factors underlying such comments. There is pressure from the demands imposed on us by our environment, peers, colleagues and family. The irony is that most of us need some of these pressures to function at our best. Other underlying factors include the consequences, physical and mental, that flow from these demands. These can include tiredness, illness, disorientation and breakdown. Such symptoms can be both recurring and very serious. Sometimes changes in our work situation cause stress – notably retirement, job change and taking on new responsibilities. All of us can also relate to stress that comes from relationships at work; from ambiguities about our role; from specific conflict situations; from our own temperaments and so on. Christians live with stresses from many different sources. Not all of church life is joyous. Personality clashes and disputes over practice and theology only serve to exacerbate the life stresses that some Christians face. Many Christians say that the greatest stresses in their lives are church related, and not from their secular work. Sometimes the high standards of behavior set out in the Bible cause Christians to feel under pressure. Even reading Christian books, like this one, that draw these matters to their attention can cause stress! This is a difficult area, and the solution is not to offer trite and neatly packaged solutions. Usually we need to tackle both the source and the symptoms. And, to go back to where we started, we regularly need God's confirmation that we are in the right job. While joy and peace can be scarce commodities, finding them again is essential.[4] As the psalmist

> I am convinced that I am in the job God wants me to do. But why is it so very stressful?

says, "When I was in distress, I sought the Lord; at night I stretched out untiring hands and my soul refused to be comforted".[5]

Identity Finally, I want to touch briefly on the issue of identity and self-esteem. Work can also generate extremes in this area. Too much ego can breed pride and independence; too little can be both negative and destructive. This lack of identity can leave people stranded, without an evident place in society. Many of us use the role we do (or did, or aspire to) at work as a way of introducing ourselves to others. Remarks such as, "I am a plumber"; "I was a teacher"; "I plan to be a doctor" all testify to the importance we attach to our roles. People without employment often struggle with a sense of identity and have a sense of failure, a simmering anger and a lack of confidence. Christians are not exempt from such emotions. On the other hand, an excess of ego is often expressed in arrogance, pride and a cynical disregard for others. Both extremes show unhealthy relations with the concept of work. We may well not understand what has happened to us professionally, or why. But we cannot glorify God in our work, whatever that may be, if our sense of self is distorted. If we are full of ourselves and our own importance, or if we have no confidence, the result is the same. We are not acknowledging that our sense of self needs to come from God – from our creation in his image and from our redemption by Christ on the cross. Jesus pointed out the damaging effects of both these extremes. The Pharisees were at one extreme, the woman at the well at the other. Our self-esteem rests solely on God's grace – not on where our pay comes from, the size of our office or the length of our entry in *Who's Who*. The psalmist encourages all of us with these words, "You made him (humankind) a little lower than the heavenly beings and crowned him with glory and honor".[6] We should not, of course, confuse the need to know ourselves and be confident as to who we are with biblical teaching on self-denial. Jesus was very clear in his call to the disciples, "If anyone would come after me, he must deny himself and take up his cross daily and follow me".[7]

☑ **ACTION:** Are some of these paradoxes, or perhaps others, currently affecting your own work life or your perspective on work? Which do you find most difficult and why? It has been said that the Lord didn't burden us with work: he blessed us with it. In your current work situation, can you honestly say that you agree with that?

While we can comment on these paradoxes in general, we can't solve them here. All of us need to resolve them at a personal level by revisiting some of what was said in the first two chapters. For example, if you struggle with work and time, consider honestly whether your approach to both of these brings God glory. This follows the route of obedience, rather than asking someone for a formula or an algorithm to make your work life better. If we look for the biblical answer, we will find that God wants honor in our personal, family, church, work and community lives.[8] Many Christians have shelves full of books on work-life balance that have made no difference whatsoever to their lives – not because they can't read, but because they don't obey. The only person who can really fix these problems is God, through the power of his Spirit.

The Bible is the only book that teaches us what a healthy Christian life is like

But we have to be willing to do what he says. When God called us, he did not ask us to join a cafeteria line and pick up the parts of the Christian menu that pleased us. If we are to bring God glory, we may need to resolve some paradoxes associated with our personal work – and fast. The Bible is the only book that teaches us what a healthy Christian life is like. We ignore it at our peril.

What's happening to work?

The aim of this section is not to gaze into a crystal ball, however fascinating that might be. We will, rather, reflect on how Christians are to respond to the ever-shifting world of work with their timeless values. For years, experts have been heralding a workplace revolution. In essence, they describe the following scenario: jobs for life are dead; many more jobs are flexible; the pace of work is accelerated; white collar jobs become a thing of the past; and everything of significance for volume employment moves to countries where costs are much lower. As a consequence of some of these trends, people are said to be tiring of long hours of commuting; work-life relationships are in serious imbalance; and more people are either opting out of work altogether or seeking self-employment in the hope that it will bring a lifestyle of choice. Taken together, these trends are often referred to as "the transformation of work", and they have been keeping publishers and pundits alike busy for years. Many of these trends will strike a chord with us. They will confirm what we feel and see. But, in fact, a number of them have actually been happening much more slowly that we have been led to believe. Others changes, such as self-employment, working from home and more frequent job changes, are growing more in perception than in reality.

All of this is not to deny that we live in times of unprecedented change in terms of many of the variables that determine the nature of work. The heightened pace of scientific discovery and technological change, for example, is likely to demand higher levels of education and training, generate much new employment and further transform the way we work. As innovation accelerates and becomes more geographically widespread, competitive conditions will intensify for many industries. Meanwhile, medical knowledge is doubling approximately every five years, and unprecedented ethical issues therefore abound. The Internet is growing both exponentially and globally, with all kinds of positive and negative implications. Both management and employees will have to come to terms with lifelong learning in such an environment – at a social and economic cost. New graduates today might expect to have up to five or six different careers, depending on life expectancy and retirement age. Two-income families are already the norm in many developed economies, and work practices are likely to have to adjust even more to this reality. For these and other reasons, birthrates have already declined in many of these countries. On the business side, companies will have to reshape themselves even more frequently, as they come to terms with globalization. No business is now too large to be a takeover target – and so the uncertainty multiplies. In all of this, time is becoming the world's most precious commodity.

We are often told that the workplace of the twenty-first century requires a different set of skills and a different kind of leader from those needed in the "industrial age". This line of argument usually goes on to say that in economies where knowledge, creativity and innovation are prized, people are the "bottom line" and their potential must be harnessed, rather than instructed. Although I live in a world where these attributes are prized, I don't see much evidence of these attitudes. You probably don't see it either. In a similar vein, the new employment era is supposed to be one of flexible, non-bureaucratic organizations in which people have more power to choose employment opportunities and to negotiate terms and conditions. In this world, employability replaces employment security as the basis for employment contracts. But there are significant gaps between this rhetoric and the reality of employment for many people. Meanwhile, many surveys show that work

many surveys show that work dominates people's lives to the detriment of other interests, including family

dominates people's lives to the detriment of other interests, including family; that they want to alter this pattern; that they are searching for work-life balance and so on.[9] But I don't meet large numbers of people, including Christians, with the will to actually change their life priorities or patterns to achieve any of these longed-for goals.

No one knows for certain what the future of work will be. But some of the present trends clearly do concern Christians. Over recent years, I have discussed work issues with lots of different people who follow Christ. They communicate much confusion and many different emotions about their world of work. Some of their uncertainty concerns the future, but much of it is about the present. For many, and for various personal reasons, work feels different. Perhaps we can make better sense of work by asking "why?". Here are some of the reasons Christians give.

Risk and uncertainty These come in various guises. Work is less secure than it once was for many people. Employment tenure is one reason, others include not being perceived to be ambitious enough, having preoccupying interests "external" to work and skills becoming obsolete.

Change The chosen careers of many people have changed in ways that make them question why they are there. Many people feel uncomfortable in an increasingly competitive and aggressive work environment. Some of these changes call for greater time commitments or for them to be rather different kinds of people.

Individualism The spirit of the age promotes teamwork but lauds individualism. This is difficult for some Christians because it is self-seeking. Others feel that it smacks of "new age" and have difficulties when it is built into some of the personal development programs they are required to undergo. Finding yourself becomes more important than finding God.

Performance Christians aspire, or should aspire, to excellence in their work. In many contexts, excellence is being redefined. For example, it often includes high time demands outside working hours; infinite flexibility in work patterns; implicitly measuring performance by hours at work beyond the stated norm; being of necessity a "corporate" person who gives all to the organization and so on.

Morality The dramatic change in attitudes to sex has affected the workplace and has many implications for working relationships. Christians need to exercise care and show greater wisdom than ever in these areas. Even when values are discussed, they are set out in morally neutral terms. They sound persuasive, but often they are not put into practice. For some, the workplace is a morality-free zone.

Pollution There is a danger that, as values are discounted and faith as a basis for life is further discarded, Christians can become more and more like the people they work with – by a process of drift. Part of this is the struggle for many to be salt and light when the people to whom they witness have no framework into which to fit Christianity. Another dimension of this insidious pollution is the worship of the god of materialism.

> ☑ **ACTION:** Consider the concerns you have about making sense of your work – in the present or as you think about the direction in which it seems to be going. In doing so, you may add to the list of six areas cited above – or completely change them. Which of these issues are the most pressing for you at the present time? And how are you trying to resolve them?

Is there a Christian way of making sense of work?

While the modern workplace can be both demanding and confusing for Christians, it is where God has placed us. Some of its many anomalies involve us; others are evident around us. Both can be equally perplexing. We are puzzled about the highly trained person who has skills in abundance but no steady employment, and the multi-skilled individual who is repeatedly made redundant. What about that Christian friend who does not know where to turn, and for whom every work-related door closes? What about the completely immoral neighbor who always prospers at work? How can we accept the dishonest, deceitful and incompetent colleague who has cheated her way to the top? And what of the migrant worker, driven by economic imperatives, whose lifestyle is beyond your comprehension because he faces long-term, often indefinite, separation from family and friends? Or the two parents who work on opposite shifts for forty weeks a year and rarely see their family together? Or the person in the next estate who works by satellite only and never sees a colleague other than by video conference? How about the executive who goes New York and Tokyo alternate weeks for meetings and often does 80,000 air miles per month – and who claims to be fulfilled by all of this? These are just a few examples of the world of work in which Christians live.

Interesting though all such cases may be, what is essential is that we make Christian sense of our own personal work. How do we do that in the midst of all of life's demands? How do I know that what I do "fits in" with God's purpose for me? To address these and other related questions, let me encourage you to think in the following way. As my career has progressed, I have found that making sense of my daily work depends on ...

Perspective The place from which I am viewing it. Viewed from the hustle and bustle of everyday life, it is very difficult to see work clearly. We live in the world of the "perpetual now". The immediate crushes in; the deadlines and priorities are dominant; the stresses and strains of relationships are only too real; and there is always risk and uncertainty. We need to consider God's perspective. Why did he lead me here? Why he is keeping me here? What is it that he wants done while I am here? What does my work look like, viewed from heaven? Does God get enough (or any) space to give me his perspective on my work? Seeing ourselves from God's perspective often requires that we are still – one of the hardest things to achieve in modern life.

Vision The eyes through which we see ourselves and our work are crucial. It's easy for all of us to see our work in the classic terms as earning a living, providing for our families and so on. But when God looks at your work, what does he see? Does he see faith? Witness? Love? Or does he see total commitment to every possible priority other than his own? Inconsistency of practice? A reluctance to identify with his kingdom? Knowing how God sees us would surely challenge our behavior.

Spirit What is the condition of your heart as you look at your life and work? What are your attitudes to God? Are you willing to hear and obey? Are you open to redirection? Often this boils down to what we are trying to achieve in our work. What's in your heart about your work? Are you planning to maximize money, status, promotion, reputation and so on? And how does that compare to what God wants you to achieve? Have you made a point of asking him? And, frankly, does God have any place in your attitude to work?

These three categories for making sense of work have several common features. They are all spiritual exercises; they are independent of the present and future shape of work; they apply to all work situations; and they are all about the lordship of Christ in our work. As the theme text for this chapter points out, making sense of work is only possible if we set apart Christ as Lord – giving to him the reverence and respect that is his due. The following section reinforces the importance of these points with some biblical lessons on how God speaks in the stillness – provided we are willing to be there to hear him.

Making sense while being still

There is much evidence that the pressures that come from work affect a Christian's stillness. The effects may not be evident on the surface. Many of us are experts at masking inner turmoil with external calm; while others claim to rejoice in the inner peace of God while visibly living with a high degree of anxiety. For others, life in general, and work in particular are associated with neither external nor internal stillness. The Bible makes it clear that God would have it otherwise. So the Lord said to Israel, "In repentance and rest is your salvation, in quietness and trust is your strength, but you would have none of it".[10] That's the problem for many of us. It's not that God hasn't provided. It's rather that we don't want to know. How does a passage like "the peace of God, which transcends all understanding, will guard your hearts and your minds in Christ Jesus"[11] relate to your attitude to your daily work? Perhaps not at all. For most of us, peace and work don't fit into the same sentence. God, however, promised to bless his people as he led them to stillness in some very unlikely circumstances.

Many of us are experts at masking inner turmoil with external calm

Be still – to be delivered The Israelites were under intense pressure. Having just left Egypt, they were terrified as an army marched towards them to take them back. The Egyptians had quickly decided that to allow this ready supply of slaves to leave was an economic disaster. Ahead of them lay the Red Sea. They were in turmoil, critical of their leaders, fabricating rosy memories of how good life really had been in Egypt, acting as if they were on their own. Sound familiar? In that unlikely context, the word from Moses was, "The LORD will fight for you; you need only to be still".[12] Humanly speaking, being still at precisely that moment in their lives was improbable. It was the last thing on their minds. Many of us would have been building rafts or testing out our long-distance swimming abilities. Yet it was in that situation, and through their subsequent rescue by the parting of the waters, that God assured them that he would "gain glory".[13] The moral of this incident? No stillness, no glory. As M. Eckhart observed several centuries ago, "Nothing in all creation is so like God as stillness."

Be still – to be instructed We all need to have a refreshed perspective. To a group of people who seemed to have forgotten how God had blessed them in the past and preserved them through natural and political disasters, David brought God's message. "Be still, and know that I am God."[14] They were encouraged to have supreme confidence in the promise of God's ultimate sovereignty. And so are we. But first their memories had to be stirred. And so do ours. It's usually best done in stillness. In this setting, being still enabled God's people to recall his track record in their lives, to remember who he really was and to re-establish their faith in his future purpose.

Be still, and know that I am God.

Be still – to be restored G.K. Chesterton once said, "The one spiritual disease is thinking that one is quite well". So it was with Elijah, in that his greatest trial came shortly after his one of his greatest triumphs. He had just defeated the prophets of Baal before King Ahab with an impressive display of God's power. Now he was on the run from Jezebel, in fear for his life. He assumed that he was the only prophet left, and consequently he bore all kinds of burdens that were not his to bear. God's challenge to him was, "What are you doing here, Elijah?".[15] Told to stand on the mountain to witness God's presence, he found that it was not in the wind, earthquake or the fire, but in "a gentle whisper".[16] It was a voice that could only be heard in the stillness. The experience on the mountain was calculated to allow him to experience God's presence again, to recalibrate his life to God's power again, and to give answers to God's questions as to what he was doing with his life. We need to be able to do all three of these as well if we are to understand the answer to the question, "Whose work is it anyway?". We will consider this incident in Elijah's life in greater depth in Chapter 8.

The examples above illustrate how foundational stillness is to our lives in general, and to our working lives in particular. But more than that, as we see in the examples above, we also need deliverance, instruction and restoration in order to keep making sense of our work. We need deliverance from its pervasive demands, from the priorities of the world and from the temptation to think that it is ours, not God's. We need instruction on God's perspective to prevent us from making complex what is simple in his eyes. And we need restoration from the tendency to think that we are alone when trying to find the right relationship with both our work and our God. Edna Becker's poem helps to direct us to the imperative that is stillness.

If, like the lake that has the boon
Of cradling the little moon
Above the hill
I want the Infinite to be
Reflected undisturbed in me,
I must be still

Challenge No3

Try to find a way of being still as you reflect on this chapter. That might be a tall order if you are on a commuter train, on your coffee break in a machine shop, with the children at home or in any number of situations that seem far from stillness. But try to find a still time soon and reflect on the following:

1 What aspects of your work do you find difficult to make sense of? And why?

2 Is Jesus Christ the Lord of your work? In what ways does that show, in your own heart and in the work environment?

3 Many readers will be confused and have fears and uncertainties about their roles in the world of work. Spend some time prayerfully applying the concepts of perspective, vision and spirit.

4 How can you build more stillness into your pattern of life?

Further reading

Anderson, Jock, *In the Stillness* (Carlisle: Alpha, 1999).

Lucado, Max, *Let the Journey Begin: God's Roadmap for New Beginnings* (Nashville: Word, 1998).

Packer, J.I., *Rediscovering Holiness* (Ann Arbor, MI: Servant, 1992).

Stott, John, *The Incomparable Christ* (Leicester: IVP, 2001).

Endnotes

1 Heb. 13:8.

2 Charles Handy, *The Empty Raincoat* (London: Arrow, 1995), p. 26.

3 Col. 3:17.

4 A very helpful discussion on this topic is to be found in Westcott, *Work Well: Live Well* (London: Marshall Pickering, 1994), Chapter 6.

5 Ps. 77:2.

6 Ps. 8:5.

7 Lk. 9:23.

8 See passages such as Col. 3 and Eph. 6 on these topics.

9 The scope of this chapter precludes a deeper examination of these trends in the world of work. You might wish to look further into them in books such as the following: P. Rayman, *Beyond the Bottom Line: The Search for Dignity at Work* (New York: St. Martin's Press, 2001); J. Ciulla, *The Working Life: The Promise and Betrayal of Modern Work* (New York: Times, 2000); L. Worrall and C. Cooper, *The Quality of Working Life* (London: Institute of Management, 1999).

10 Isa. 30:15.

11 Phil. 4:7.

12 Ex. 14:14.

13 Ex. 14:17.

14 Ps. 46:10.

15 1 Kgs. 19:9.

16 1 Kgs. 19:12.

PART THREE
LEARNING THROUGH THE PRACTICE OF OUR WORK

4
Danger – Christians at Work

"The LORD does not look at the things man looks at. Man looks at the outward appearance, but the LORD looks at the heart." (1 Sam. 16:7)

Outline   Throughout Part 3, we will consider Christian practice at work. Chapters 4 and 5 begin with a series of health warnings about dangers and conflicts. As we have seen, God designed work to be positive, but it does have built-in hazards. The three dangers discussed below are only a few of the many that are possible to identify. They reflect my own experience both as a participant in, and an observer of, the world of work.

What dangers?
This introductory section establishes that the Christian really does face dangers associated with work.

Applying New Age thinking to our work
In a brief review of this phenomenon, we evaluate the way in which it has influenced much of this generation's perspective on work and how it can subtly seep into Christian thought.

Failing to be a witness at work
The four cases in this section illustrate some of the many challenges that Christians face when witnessing in the workplace. This section also addresses the widespread and highly damaging issue of hypocrisy.

▶

Making a god out of a career
We see here that each of us is capable of gradually sliding from displaying good Christian discipleship in work to making our work a god. This section also sets out the characteristics of idol worship.

A matter of relationships
We conclude the chapter by acknowledging that the only known Christian antidote to these hazards is to revisit our relationship with the Lord. Is it rich or poor? We learn from the experience of Psalm 63.

What dangers? Having laid the foundations and stressed the need to make Christian sense of our work, we now need to face up to some of the hazards associated with the competitive work environment in which many of us operate. While all of us recognize an element of futility in our work, this is especially painful for the person who is not a follower of Christ. Work-related glamor and successes are short-lived. Above all else, sin has a major impact on our co-workers (both Christian and non-Christian), and therefore affects our relationships. And we ourselves are far from exempt from its wiles. John Blanchard was right when he said, "we are born in sin and spend our lives coping with the consequences". As a result, there are many sin-induced dangers at work. Dangers and opportunities, however, are often quite closely linked. The Chinese characters for both are identical – literally, crisis is "an opportunity riding the dangerous wind". So Christians can find that circumstances which carry a serious threat at work may also generate enormous opportunities. The environmental effects of sin on work are all around us. Sin has made work harder and brought many frustrations and conflicting emotions. But, at the same time, the broken and dysfunctional lives of colleagues often open their eyes to the need for faith. Similarly, we can try to turn situations of conflict into positive outcomes or bring some form of assistance to our peers in the midst of crises. While the three hazards discussed below are quite far-reaching in their implications, they may not be particular sources of danger for you. But think twice (or three times) if you don't consider that there are any dangers associated with your work. We will deal more fully with the opportunities that these dangers present later in the book, in Chapters 6, 9 and 10.

☑ **ACTION:** As you read the following section, think about the particular dangers that you face at work. Make a list of them. And then try to fit them into the three categories below. To what conclusions does this exercise lead you?

The Bible gives us good grounds for being on guard in our work. Jesus assumed the implicit dangers when he sent out the 12 disciples. "I am sending you out like sheep among wolves. Therefore be as shrewd as snakes and as innocent as doves".[1] Paul reflected this attitude with the advice, "Do everything without complaining or arguing, so that you may become blameless and pure, children of God without fault in a crooked and depraved generation, in which you shine like stars in the universe as you hold out the word of life".[2] This is quite an assessment of our context, and a challenging job specification! Do you think that you are fulfilling its terms? Think about just how much expectation of danger is built into that advice. It is also important to remember that Jesus said, "If the world hates you, keep in mind that it hated me first".[3] These verses add to our understanding of God's perspective on our work – an issue that we noted as vital in Chapter 3.

Looking more closely at some of the dangers associated with work is like switching on the lights in the lighthouse. We are familiar with the waters, but not with all the hazards. There is a chart, but we don't always consult it. Life on the ship is busy, and everyone is preoccupied. The Master is on the ship somewhere, but not always at the helm – because we like to share the steering. And there are rocks in abundance.

Applying New Age thinking to our work

Pause to reflect before you protest that this is not one of your personal dangers. You might contend, "I have no idea what this is, and no interest in knowing". Or perhaps, "I've never knowingly met someone with such ideas – don't they dress up in strange clothes, have dreadlocks and hug trees?". Some do, but most don't. And there are a lot of people with such ideas in business suits, thinly disguised as your colleagues. That's part of the problem. Few of us have enough time to study every passing fad in world thinking. But we all breathe the same air, and it's full of strange ideas that erode the Christian view of life and work. We are all probably unknowing victims of it. We started to meet New Age ideas in

Chapter 1 when we were looking at the prevailing worldview of work. It is an intrinsic part of the "spirit of our age".

New Age is an umbrella term, connecting a whole series of disparate movements that attempt to underpin a vast array of different lifestyles.[4] The name "New Age" comes from the astrological theory that presumes that each star lasts for 2000 years. The Age of Pisces (the fish symbol of Christianity) has passed, we are told, and we are now in the Age of Aquarius. New Age is a powerful mixture of mysticism, nature religions and the occult – often packaged as a very soft sell. Many bookstores are full of its literature, and the pervasive presence of its ideas in the media has made a huge impact in many walks of life – from schools to airport executive lounges. The best summary of the disparate beliefs of New Age that I have read is that by John Stott when he describes it as: "All is God", "All is one", and "All is well". In this way of thinking, for example, God is not a person but a creative force; the way to find him is to look within ourselves, not in the Bible; the priority in life is to find our own self at whatever cost. The only salvation in New Age is self-salvation. The route to success is self-realization. There are no moral absolutes, and guidance in all things comes from within. The net effect is to underpin a set of lifestyles in which "anything goes". By its tolerance of all views, it implicitly erodes the mandate to follow Jesus Christ as Lord. In fact, New Age constitutes a root and branch challenge to all aspects of our Trinitarian faith. Christian belief is seen as ill-founded, too narrow, not sufficiently open to new ideas and ultimately a delusion. New Age thinking can seriously damage Christian health.

The only salvation in New Age is self-salvation

I recently had a fascinating experience in the London Underground. The train compartment was relatively quiet, and two ladies near me were in earnest conversation about their eclectic New Age reading. Having covered recent horoscopes, lifestyle choices in their personal affairs and some aspects of the occult, one of them reached into her bag and produced a copy of *Mere Christianity* by C.S. Lewis. "There's great new age thinking in this", she said, "all about liberating the person." The other readily agreed, and asked her if she had read any of Max Lucado's work. "There's some really good material in these Christian bookstores, you know" was her conclusion. There is bad news and good news here in this story. On the one hand, people view

Christianity as just part of a cocktail of ideas and as having nothing unique to say. On the other hand, God can use people's openness to Christian ideas and to reading Christian literature to bring them to Christ.

For the Christian church, such a "pick and mix" approach to beliefs is not a new problem. A verse such as "See to it that no-one takes you captive through hollow and deceptive philosophy"[5] could have been written last week about life in the twenty-first century. The Greco-Roman world of the first century shared many common characteristics with ours. Surrounded with such a clutch of philosophies, Timothy was advised to "keep your head in all situations".[6] The following is a summary of some of the more obvious current New Age dangers to our Christian way of thinking about work.

My work is mine. I do it my way, for my ends. It has nothing to do with a calling from anyone else, because nobody else matters.

Whatever your relationship with work is, it is just fine. It should not be subject to challenge from higher authority – because you are the only authority that counts.

Your work doesn't matter to God. You are a witness to your own journey; love is a detached and vague concept; and you are working for your glory.

If work makes sense to you, that's all that matters. Forget God's perspective – he has much less right to one than you have. After all, it's your life!

☑ **ACTION:** Honestly appraise how you think about work in a Christian way. Consider whether some of the above attitudes have not on occasion infiltrated into your own thinking. There are moments in all of our more tense working days when some of this might sound quite appealing. You may find that such ideas have crept in at particular moments, although perhaps you did not know where they came from. In Paul's farewell to the Ephesian elders, he warns them, "I know that after I leave, savage wolves will come in among you and will not spare the flock".[7] Pray that God will preserve you from wolves of all types, including those that come in sheep's clothing.

Failing to be a witness at work We saw in both Chapters 1 and 2 that God calls Christians to be witnesses at work. James S. Stewart expressed this in forceful terms. "The real problem of Christianity is not atheism or scepticism, but the non-witnessing Christian trying to smuggle his own soul into heaven." Ouch, that hurts! We should first acknowledge what is involved in witnessing. Much of witnessing involves love in action – being Christ-like in character, showing forth the fruits of the Spirit and, of course, looking for the opportunity to tell others about the good news of Jesus Christ. Jesus summarized this lifestyle when he said, "In the same way, let your light shine before men, that they may see your good deeds and praise your Father in heaven."[8] All of us live and work in very different situations. But let's begin with the assumption that there are few better places than the workplace for a non-Christian to see the difference that Christ does (or does not) make in the lives of his followers. One of the best ways to explore this whole area is to look at the following representative cases and ask what they say to us and what dangers they highlight. And we will look at how closely witnessing is linked to Christian character in Chapter 6, where we consider discipleship at work.

All of us live and work in very different situations

Four case studies: Christian witness at work

● *Michael – the separatist.* Michael was a youth leader and a Christian. At age forty he was also the highly successful manager of a local electronics company. In his role as youth leader he had recently written letters to parents whose children attended his club, seeking written permission for their teenagers' attendance at summer camp. Joe, one of his line supervisors at work, had children in Michael's club and had received a copy of this letter. Joe wanted clarification about health and safety at the camp, the qualifications and experience of the leaders and so on before he agreed to let his two sons go. He was really delighted that Michael's church was taking an interest in his boys, and he was amazed that someone of Michael's caliber was giving time to this. Joe didn't have any personal interest in God, but he was determined to let his family choose their own way in life. In fact, the summer camp was only one of the reasons why he asked for an appointment to talk with Michael. Joe had some problems with his marriage and, knowing that his boss was a Christian, he wanted some advice. He had never spoken to anyone about these problems before. Joe had a lot of respect for Michael, who was rather remote from the workforce but respected for his open style of management and his fairness. An appointment was made. Michael was very pleasant, and he satisfactorily explained the details of the camp over a cup of coffee. However, when the real reason for the meeting emerged, he reacted rather differently. "I'm sorry, Joe, I don't talk about personal matters with the staff – have you spoken to the human resources team? Or what about coming to our church on Sunday? Our pastor is great on marriage. This is a matter of principle for me." Joe thought that the Bible said something about love and care for others; he left both embarrassed and disillusioned. He vowed that he would never look for help in that direction again.

● *Bill – the hypocrite*. Bill was a bully at school and had been one ever since. He was a rather volatile person, very competitive, and he always dominated conversations at work and leisure. He was not popular – as the annual office party games revealed. Everybody in the office had views about Bill, and they were not all bad. He could be very kind, but when he was he made sure that everybody knew about it. He was rumored to be a churchgoer, but people were all a bit vague about where and when. Overall, he was not a bad colleague, unless you were a woman. Basically, he thought women were less able at work than men – and he thought that political correctness was a way of keeping accurate election scores. Worst of all, he sometimes made sexually inappropriate comments and Mary, who had joined the company six weeks ago, was the latest victim. She was a quiet, bright and attractive girl, and this was her first job after leaving college. She found Bill disgusting. On Sunday past, Mary passed a downtown church and was sure that she saw Bill go into it. He saw her too, and before she could disappear around a corner, Bill eagerly rushed out of the church to ask her if she would like to come in. "Hi Mary, this is a special week of events geared for your age group – great band, lots of smart young men." Her response to Bill is unprintable.

● *Jenny – the secret disciple*. A very competent young corporate lawyer, Jenny was just five years out of graduate school with a bright future. Her work was demanding, and long hours were just part of her job. She managed to be minimally involved in her local church, but it was tough. She regularly had to work weekends. "No way to the twelve-hour day" was the practice slogan – meaning that nothing less than fourteen would do. Jenny was a follower of Jesus Christ – a commitment that dated from a campus mission. But, as far as she could tell, there were no other Christians in the practice. She might have found that there were – if she ever had time to talk about something other than the latest takeover defense or that prospective management buyout at the other end of town. Jenny always wore a fish badge, but it was neatly tucked behind the collar of her gray suits. The opportunity to witness never seemed to arise. Then, three years later, Mark joined the practice. Jenny and he had attended the same college, where he was a real "Jesus freak". Everybody knew about his faith; he was fearless. He was so fearless, in fact, that the senior partners pondered a little at his interviews. But he was a class act, and "a bit of variety would do us all no harm" was their conclusion. They hired him. Mark was introduced to Jenny at his welcome cocktail party, "Hey Jenny, still praising the Lord, I hope!" he called from a distance. Jenny managed a positive, but scarcely audible, response. "Now there's a surprise", said the senior partner. "I'm not sure that we have room for two of you lot." Neither Mark nor Jenny quite knew what to say. And it occurred to Jenny that she now faced some real challenges in order to make her witness credible in this law firm. She saw that she was very open to a charge of hypocrisy.

The opportunity to witness never seemed to arise

● *Rachel – the quiet planter.* From the time her brothers played with toy trucks on the lawn, Rachel wanted to be in the construction industry. Her parents hoped that this crazy idea would go away; her teachers saw that it wouldn't. When she was in high school she made the decision that she was going into construction, and the marginal compromise was that she would train first as a civil engineer. Rachel kept saying that this (improbably, some thought) was God's will for her life. From the time she started site visits, she was barraged by wolf whistles and cat calls. Rachel could handle this. She was excellent at her job, and soon the leading agents were asking for her to handle their sites. She had the distinctive gift of listening to people, whether they were working cranes or digging drains. Unlikely though it might seem, men old enough to be her father would at times take a small Bible from her. She always carried them in her rucksack. She had some hard taskmasters who had little time for women on sites, let alone a Christian one. Some made her life really difficult. But her witness was effective, her seed sowing consistent. She was often asked to pray for family problems. Five years later, she changed jobs to work in a civil engineering consulting company in the same city. She and Robert planned to marry, and her construction job had recently involved too much traveling. A year later she received a letter from Carlos, who had tracked her down. He wanted to tell her that his daughter had become a Christian by reading the Bible she gave him four years previously. Her life had been in ruins and her wayward behavior had caused great distress to her parents. Her family witness had been such that he and his wife had also come to Christ. Rachel (and Robert) thanked God that they both knew the Lord of the harvest.

☑ **ACTION:** Reflect on the following questions.

Was Joe's expectation of Michael a reasonable one? Was Michael right to respond to Joe in the way he did? How else could he have handled this situation?

What is the way back for Bill in terms of his relationships with Mary and his colleagues? If Bill asked you for counseling, what advice would you give him?

How might Jenny and Mark work together to bring glory to the Lord in this company in the months ahead?

What have you learned from Rachel's story or from observing others like Rachel in the work context?

Are there any parallels between these cases and your own practice as a Christian in the workplace?

Read the theme text at the beginning of the chapter. What was going on in the hearts of the Christians involved in these cases? What do you think God's view of them would be?

There can be few greater threats to the cause of Christ than hypocrisy. So the case of Bill deserves special mention. In or out of the work context, there is no sin more roundly condemned in the New Testament. Others are quick to spot and despise hypocrisy. It's one of the easiest sins to commit, and we can all be guilty of it. And when we separate work and faith, hypocrisy is bound to occur. Somehow we think that what happens at work doesn't matter quite as much as what we are among our Christian peer group. Nothing could be further from God's truth. The Bible refers to hypocrisy of several types. Noting some of these types might help us avoid it. Hypocrisy occurs when alleged beliefs are not consistent with behavior. It can involve play-acting goodness – doing or saying things to be seen. When someone breaks God's laws in the name of religion and hides his true motives under a mask of pretense, that is hypocrisy. One of its many manifestations is when a Christian vigorously condemns sin but continues shamelessly to sin himself. Most observers find this hard to take. In the end, hypocrisy develops its own blindness and so attracts the Lord's condemnation. Referring to the returning master assessing his servants, he said, "He will cut him to pieces and assign him a place with the hypocrites, where there will be weeping and gnashing of teeth".[9] Even as you read this, you may think of cases known to you in which hypocritical behavior has been very damaging to Christian witness at work. We all need to examine our own lives and motivations.

> Hypocrisy occurs when alleged beliefs are not consistent with behavior

Making a god out of a career Our theme text for this chapter comes into its own here. In matters relating to careers, improving the "outward appearance" can be very tempting. Promotion, recognition, status and its associated trappings are the substance of success in the workplace for most of us. That's the dimension that people see – and it may be the one that we want to see, too. But such external indicators may, or may not, be part of God's plan for our lives. What is evident in 1 Samuel, and in the rest of the Bible, is that God measures us according to what is going on in the heart. This, then, is where we must focus our attention – otherwise following Christ is a hollow practice. The Lord wants us to do well at our work and to enjoy our achievements. And so doing may well lead to rapid career progression that can be to his glory. That is wholly consistent with what we learned in Chapters 1 and 2. But seeking to "do well" as an end in itself can destroy Christian life and move us from being God-honoring to being self-honoring. If we are solely focused on achieving such measures of success, we are well down the route to making a god of our careers. The problem is that, even in some Christian communities, many people place a premium on material progress, without any more than a nod in the direction of spiritual progress. The externals can look great and may impress others, but the heart may be spiritually bankrupt. We may be gilded outside but destitute inside. May God deliver us all from this.

Think carefully about the following words from the psalmist:

Not to us, O LORD, not to us but to your name be the glory, because of your love and faithfulness.[10]

I have not met many Christians who set out to make a god of their careers, but I have seen plenty of examples of this happening along the way. Few of them like to describe their relationship with work in this way. It implies excess, lack of control and a loss of a sense of perspective, and few Christians are comfortable with that. A.W. Tozer said that "an idol of the mind is as offensive to God as an idol of the hand". Work and careers can become just that – idols of the mind. We have probably all heard versions of the following. "Sure, I'm driving 150 per cent for promotion, but that's what God wants isn't it?" "When I reach the top of my mountain, I'll have a better view of the foothills – and see the rest of my life much more clearly." "People exaggerate how committed I am to my work. I've always had it fully under control – it only looks bad from the outside. The Lord understands." On the face of it, these are neither good nor bad comments. The only person who can test such statements for their "idolatry content" is God, who knows the heart. But, believe me – test them he does!

I have not met many Christians who set out to make a god of their careers

Having established that there are very real dangers here, let's pause to consider the following vital questions that we should all apply to our careers on a regular basis.

Lordship in practice. Is Jesus Christ the Lord of my career ambitions? How much conversation and consultation have I had with him about them? How often have I exposed them to the light of his words in the Bible?

Idol worship. Has my relationship with work moved into the unhealthy zone in which I worship my career more than God? Danger signs here might include an absolute preoccupation with work at all times, a desire to only talk about work and achievements and so on.

Altar call. Have I recently asked the Lord if I am doing my work in such a way that he could bless it? Does my behavior at work have, or deserve, his seal of approval?

When John wrote to the church in Ephesus and told them, "Dear children, keep yourselves from idols",[11] he probably did not have careers specifically in mind. There were few towns with more connections to the ancient gods, and no town more proud of them. So there were plenty of alternative gods around. But his advice was generic and applies to all objects of false devotion, to anything that leads Christians to abandon the real for the illusory. An idol is anything that we worship instead of God and which we allow to take the place of God. Could this be a career? Yes, it could. Could this be your career? Certainly.

As William Cowper wrote in the eighteenth century,

> *The dearest idol I have known*
> *Whate' er that idol be,*
> *Help me to tear it from thy throne,*
> *And worship only thee*

☑ **ACTION:** Having thought seriously about these three questions, let me encourage you to take this a little further. From our observations of how people around us treat idols of all kinds (money, celebrities, sports heroes, business moguls, artifacts, etc.), let's recall the ways in which idols exert influence in order to honestly question our own relationship to our careers. To do that might not be comfortable, but it is necessary. Note that there is a potential work dimension in each of the seven issues. Jesus cannot be Lord of our lives if (or while) such things are true of us.

Idols are held in reverence.

Idols are the most important thing in the worshipper's life.

Idols determine the character and standards of behavior of the worshipper – and other worshippers have a lot of influence, too.

The hero is the role model – whatever his values; and the worshipper wants to copy him.

The worshipper wants to spend more and more time with his idol – it's his prime source of satisfaction.

Worshippers are blind to everything else, and so their judgment is thereby often impaired.

Idols are a point of reference at all times. For the true worshipper, it's all he wants to talk about; how he measures others; all that he sees as having value.

A matter of relationships

The intention of this book is not solely to highlight problems. We all need solutions and some guidance as to how to avoid such hazards in our own lives. The temptation, however, is to address such issues with Band-Aids and look for short-term fixes. Taking our three topics in turn, we can easily illustrate this. Regarding the problem of New Age thinking, we might say, "I'll remove every book with such ideas from my library". Although this is a good idea, these ideas are also embedded in our culture, media and in many other secular practices. To stop reading about them is not enough – whereas to refocus on Christ as Lord is the perfect antidote. On the question of witnessing, you might think, "You make a forceful point, I'll leave some Christian literature around in the office, school or play group – this will ensure that my position is understood". This is commendable – but what about making some real changes in the way you live by taking (or making) opportunities to talk to people about Jesus, by watching your tongue, by showing love to that colleague who is unkind to you? On the question of making idols out of our careers, we might concede, "Yes, I do need to cool it a little – the job can take possession of my life at times – it always helps me when I go more regularly to the sports club". Exercise probably does help, but will that change the roots of the idolatry? I know no other solution to this but to reconsider the fundamental question of your relationship with God. This really is the heart of the matter.

One of the best illustrations that Jesus gave of a man with a work problem was in the parable of the rich farmer. Work was foremost in his mind – new barns, extended planting, better husbandry, productive gains and enhanced returns. His fertile business mind was clearly working overtime, and he was perhaps the kind of man in whom you would want to invest. But how did he relate to God? The passage concludes, "Yes, a person is a fool to store up earthly wealth but not have a rich relationship with God".[12] That's where we end this chapter, acknowledging that only a "rich relationship" can deliver us from these dangers. In this we are greatly helped by Psalm 63. David wrote this psalm in the desert, at a low point in his life. All relationships are two-way. If both parties don't participate, it just won't work. David gives us four couplets to illustrate what God provides on his side, which in turn calls for something from each of us. For clarity, the following is expressed in an "I do", "you do" format.

● *I looked; you loved.* God's person and power were there for David to see. "I have seen you in the sanctuary and beheld your power and your glory."[13] The effect of these work hazards that we have been examining is that they cloud our vision such that God becomes less visible, and ultimately invisible, to us. David looked again and saw God's love with freshness. God asked him, in return, to fully respond to this love. "Because your love is better than life, my lips will glorify you."[14] God is there. Where are we?

Our work is fundamentally part of God's provision

● *I praise; you provide.* David pledges to praise God in all dimensions of his life. How often, in the intensity of the workplace, does the praising of God disappear? A lot. We may casually note that the fun has gone from our work; with it often goes the Christian joy. For

God's part, David acknowledges that "My soul will be satisfied as with the richest of foods; with singing lips my mouth will praise you".[15] Our work is fundamentally part of God's provision. He did not design it to detract from our worship of him.

● *I remember; you renew.* The pressures of work often crowd out our time to think. What we know about God we too easily forget. Few of our co-workers would reward us for meditating – but God does. David's meditation time was in the "watches of the night". However and wherever we can, we need to make time to remember. That very process brought David its own rewards. His relationship with God was so much better as a result. "Because you are my help, I sing in the shadow of your wings."[16] Such was the benefit of God's renewal.

● *I hold on; you hold up.* There are many times when we feel the force of this couplet, and all we can do is hold on – whether in work or in any other aspect of our Christian experience. "My soul clings to you; your right hand upholds me."[17] God's response is quite amazing – he gives each of us his full attention with his powerful right hand. But how good are we at clinging?

Further reading

Howard, J. Grant, *Balancing Life's Demands* (Portland, OR: Multinomah, 1983).

Ortberg, John, *If You Want to Walk on Water, You've Got to Get Out of the Boat* (Grand Rapids: Zondervan, 2001).

Packer, J.I., *God Has Spoken* (Aylesbury: Hodder & Stoughton, 1979).

Smart, Dominic, *When We Get It Wrong* (Carlisle: Paternoster, 2001).

Endnotes

1 Mt. 10:16.

2 Phil. 2: 14-16.

3 Jn. 15:18.

4 If you would like to read further on this topic, see Caryl Matrisiana, *Gods of the New Age* (London: Marshall Pickering, 1985); Michael Green, *The Dawn of the New Age* (London: Darton, Longman & Todd, 1993); Douglas R. Groothius, *Revealing the New Age Jesus: Challenges to Orthodox Views of Christ* (Downers Grove, IL: IVP, 1990).

5 Col. 2:8.

6 2 Tim. 4:5.

7 Acts 20:29; see also verses 25 to 38.

8 Mt. 5:16.

9 Mt. 24:51.

10 Ps. 115:1.

11. 1 Jn. 5:21.

12 Lk. 12:21 (NLT).

13 Ps. 63:2.

14 Ps. 63:3.

15 Ps. 63:5.

16 Ps. 63:7.

17 Ps. 63:8.

Challenge No4

This chapter has covered many gritty and difficult matters, some of which are virtually 'no go' territory in much Christian conversation. Take a few moments to reflect on the following:

1 If the quality of our relationship with God is directly linked to our vulnerability to dangers at work, consider what this means for you. Is yours a rich relationship with God? If not, in what ways has your work damaged that relationship? Praise God if your work experiences have enhanced your relationship with him.

2 Try to identify the dangers that you have faced at work over recent months or years. Some of them may be quite different from those mentioned here. If you have not done so already, what steps can you take to enlist God's help to minimize their effects?

3 Pray about the challenge in Dan Greene's words, "Witnessing is not a spare-time occupation or a once-a-week activity. It must be a quality of life. You don't go witnessing, you are a witness". How would your current reputation at work stack up against this challenge?

4 Ask the Holy Spirit to highlight any area of your working life in which you are guilty of hypocritical behavior, ask forgiveness for it and pray for the power to both minimize the effects of past hypocrisy and avoid it in the future.

5
Conflict and the World of Work

"Do not be overcome by evil, but overcome evil with good." (Rom. 12:21)

Outline How frequently have you heard someone say, "work would be fine, were it not for the people I work with (or for)"? You probably hear a version of this quite often. We are still concerned with Christian practice here in this chapter, which accepts the reality of workplace conflict of different types and levels of severity. This chapter is based on the biblical view of the world. We will look at work conflicts in two very different dimensions – with our colleagues and with our owner – noting that an understanding of both is vital for knowing whose work it is that we engage in.

Christians, work and the world
This introduction reminds us of God's view of our present world. This in turn draws our attention to five important things that we have to remember about it as we think about conflict at work.

Conflict – with our colleagues
We begin this section by looking at some lessons from my personal experience of work-related conflict, followed by four case studies about conflict at work. Finally, we look to Proverbs for some helpful and demanding advice about how wise people should shape their relationships.

Conflict – with our owner
In looking at this dimension of conflict, we trace the ways in which Christians can be in dispute with God and thereby lose any sense of peace in their lives. We point to ways in which this can be restored and by which we can live our working lives to his glory.

Christians, work and the world In some ways I am reluctant to point to the expectation that there will be some measure of "conflict" for the Christian at work. This is because I enjoy my work – perhaps too much at times. On the whole I find my work stimulating and fulfilling, and so "conflict" is not the first thing I associate with it. I know of many other Christians for whom this is not the case – for a whole variety of reasons, many of which are beyond their control. There are difficult dimensions to this topic for all of us who are on God's payroll, because all of us do face conflicts at work at some time. As Oswald Chambers says, "life without conflict is impossible". For our purposes here, the word "conflict" incorporates a whole range of tensions, disagreements and levels of friction that at times characterize work. They may be neither violent nor continuous, but they all affect our spirits in a negative way and have the capacity to damage our witness.

life without conflict is impossible

When looking at conflict, we must begin with the biblical perspective on our world. While what we think of our world is interesting, what God thinks is much more important. The word the New Testament uses most frequently to refer to "the world" has a strong connotation of "order". Indeed, the biblical sequence of God's work – order (in creation), disorder (through sin), redemption (in Christ), new order – involves the harmonious integration of various (and at times hostile) elements and energies. The ultimate aim is to unite all things in Christ. We may not immediately think of disorder and rebellion as being the backdrop to our world and work environment, but God does. The following verses personalize and sum up this situation, "the sinful mind is hostile to God. It does not submit to God's law, nor can it do so. Those controlled by the sinful nature cannot please God".[1] This being the case, how are Christians to relate to this world? You might well say, "We can't hope to get anywhere as witnesses in the world if we are in constant conflict with people". That's correct, and Jesus was not in such constant conflict. But he recognized only too clearly the reality of the world he loved, and the character of the people for whom he died. He also experienced a great deal of hostility in his work – from expected and unexpected quarters. What, then, do we need to remember about our world as we look for the answer to the question "Whose work is it anyway?" and, in particular, as we address the topic of this chapter? I would suggest five things.

● *Understand the present reality*. We should not miss the presumption behind Jesus' prayer to his Father for the disciples, "I have given them your word and the world has hated them, for they are not of the world any more than I am of the world".[2] Yet this prayer was not for their removal from the world, but for their protection in it. We must thank God for his understanding and provision here, for we know that we need his protection.

● *Be aware of our own history*. We need to remember what we came from, how recently, and the effects of the hangover from the past. Here's one way of remembering. "As for you, you were dead in your transgressions and sins, in which you used to live when you followed the ways of this world and of the ruler of the kingdom of the air, the spirit who is now at work in those who are disobedient."[3] We should be confident about our salvation while remaining aware of our weakness. Our strength is, like Paul's, made perfect in weakness.

We should be confident about our salvation while remaining aware of our weakness

● *Read the health warnings*. There are many such warnings that apply to our work. They include the caution against entanglement, "No-one serving as a soldier gets involved in civilian affairs – he wants to please his commanding officer"[4] and an acknowledgment that it's easy to fall in love with this world, "Demas, because he loved this world, has deserted me ..."[5] In the context of the shortage of time, we also find wise counsel to avoid being sucked in by the world. Rather, we should be like "those who use the things of the world, as if not engrossed in them".[6] That's exactly where most of us want to be with our work – but we rarely are.

● *Realize that it is not neutral*. Our peers may at times seem indifferent to our Christian faith, but the world is not. I am much struck by Jim Packer's interpretation of the verse, "For everything in the world – the cravings of sinful man, the lust of his eyes and the boasting of what he has and does – comes not from the Father but from the world".[7] As we have seen, he calls these "the pleasure, profit, power and promotion motives". It is very easy to pursue all of these motives to excess – so we must remember their origins and not be deceived. Decorate them as we might, soften them as we may, this is the reality of our world – and God sees it as it really is.

● *Live positively within it.* With all of the above in mind, we should celebrate the great truth that one telling proof that we are Christians is that we can overcome the world – just as Jesus did: "... for everyone born of God has overcome the world. This is the victory that has overcome the world, even our faith".[8] We are both called and empowered to live victorious Christian lives in the full knowledge of the nature of our fallen world. But we always need to be able to see the world through God's eyes – otherwise we will lose our way. Speaking to our hopes and aspirations as Christians, C.S. Lewis was right to advise, "Aim at heaven and you will get earth thrown in; aim at earth and you will get neither".

In concluding this introduction to the context in which we face conflict, I am reminded of the wise words of John Stott about the hazards of "double listening"[9] – namely listening to both the word and the world. Stott notes that we have to hear the one with humble reverence, anxious to understand and obey, and the other with critical alertness. We need to pray that God will help us to distinguish between the quality of advice from these sources.

☑ **ACTION:** Take some time to review your own relationship with the world in the light of these five observations. For example, have you been assuming that the effects of the world on you are neutral and passive? Are these "health warnings" shaping your attitudes in the way in which God intends? Pray about the advice in our theme text from Romans 12 as it applies to your work environment.

Conflict – with our colleagues We all experience conflict with our colleagues from time to time. We have probably all asked the question, "What is the God-honoring way to handle this (present) conflict?". Who has not wrestled with directing the principles of Christian love towards a bitter, aggressive and spiteful colleague? Who has not wondered if the fruit of the Spirit was evident in our lives when we were in intense disagreement at work over a matter of principle? We need to accept, first of all, that we don't get exemption from Christian fundamentals in such situations. The three characteristics of what it is to be a Christian remain unchanged – namely believing, doing and being. We cannot have

Christian "dressing down" days at work when we leave salt and light in the closet at home, when grace is parked in the next county, and when love is coming in next week's mail. As has been wisely said, an account of our faith is an account of our lives. All of the principles set down in Chapters 1 and 2 apply to our work in times of conflict as well as in times of peace.

I have had much personal experience with this difficult subject. It is important to remember that not all disagreements and debates at work lead to conflict – nor should they. It is essential to encourage open communication and discussion to avoid building up negative feelings that place serious stress and strain on relationships. Reason and rational behavior, however, are singularly absent in times of intense conflict. They are absent, that is, except in the Christian heart – where the Spirit lives. But the Spirit's presence may not be evident. At times it can be difficult to remember that he is there, and it is Satan's business to help us forget it. In general, I have not lived my working life "in conflict" with my colleagues – although I have met some Christians who have. Indeed, their autobiographical milestones consist of triumphs in past work conflicts – tales of their victories, in effect! I've never been content with this approach to life, which suggests that personal gain and a form of sustenance come from the pain of others. A better starting point for the Christian is to distinguish between conflict creation and conflict resolution. Surely our focus should be on the latter wherever possible, and we should be known for our ability to assist in such resolution. It is hard to see, for example, how a Christian can be either working in partnership with God or living to bring him glory if he is known at work for being a perpetual source of conflict. This is where the proper meaning of Christian meekness – namely strength under discipline – comes in. For a Christian to be accused of being diplomatic, a peacemaker and willing to resolve workplace conflicts is no bad thing – even though those qualities may be interpreted as weakness. We should recall Jesus' radical teaching on the attitudes to be fostered in his disciples.[10]

I am not naïve about any of this. I face many situations at work that draw me into conflict, and there are many more that would if I did not purposefully try to defuse them. Because I abhor idleness and poor performance, dislike pretentious and arrogant people, have a distaste for lack of truthfulness and

> *not all disagreements and debates at work lead to conflict – nor should they*

transparency and tend to "suffer fools badly" in all walks of life, these are things that draw me into conflict. Also, I truly detest seeing junior people or individuals low down in a hierarchy being poorly treated by their bosses. On occasion I come across personalities that I could easily clash with – because we are such very different people. I am a rather direct individual, and although I have a slow fuse and do not get angry too quickly, I do express my opinions quite forcefully. When I was younger, some of my real conflicts were with people who tried to manage me, and who (in my youthful opinion) were less than competent, had few leadership qualities and made bad decisions. Looking back on my own past, I can identify some simple principles for managing through conflicts at work. Some of these are listed below.

1. *Let God take control of the conflict.* People have different personalities, but there is much to be said for not flaring up immediately, controlling our tongues and praying about the situation earlier rather than later – this includes praying for the other person or persons. Anger too often takes control of our thoughts, words and actions. The danger is that we sometimes fail to see that the Lord has a vested interest in how a work problem is going to be resolved.

2. *Resolving conflicts.* Christians often lead the way in solving conflicts at work – either because it is their job, or because they have the inner inclination to do so. Either way, the end of a conflict in a work context (in a fallen world) is not always peace – it can be merely the absence (or deferral) of strife. The challenge is to show Christian grace through the process and in the aftermath. That's not easy.

3. *Things to avoid.* Christians are to avoid using abusive language, sending rage-filled e-mails and dictating wrathful memos in the heat of a conflict situation. Neither should we allow situations to develop to the point where conflict is inevitable – the ongoing relationships at work may not matter to others, but they do to Christians. We should not think, either, that we are on our own but know how to ask advice, share with trusted people and seek a mentor. The final thing to avoid is thinking that conflict at work does not matter to God. If we are in partnership with him, it matters a great deal.

> The final thing to avoid is thinking that conflict at work does not matter to God

4. *Ask God what he is trying to teach you*. This is the tough part. In principle, I recognize that God can use a difficult and stressful work experience to shape our character. But, in the thick of it, that is not always easy to accept. But I agree, if somewhat reluctantly, with the point made by Erwin Lutzer, "More is at stake than your personal victory. Conflict is the main ingredient in God's character development programme". I confess that sometimes I rather wish it wasn't.

> ☑ **ACTION:** Take time out to think about the sources of conflict in your work, your behavior in the midst of such situations and how the four principles above apply to your own experience. Have you been able to bring God glory in any of these conflict situations – in the short term or the longer term?

Cases of conflict at work

Conflicts come in all shapes and sizes. In the four cases below, consider the behavior patterns of the Christians concerned and ask what lessons you could learn from them – both positive and negative. Try to cast yourself in the role of an adviser to Nigel and Mary. The cases of David and William and Alex and Fred introduce the added dimension of Christians working together in secular work. What can you learn from their behavior?

● *Nigel and Frank – testing God's plans*. Nigel was a successful young academic – not quite at the top of the ladder but, in the opinion of some, too young to be promoted further. He was a Christian and had no interest in academic politics. When a new senior post in his department was advertised, his colleagues encouraged him to apply. An influential member of the interview panel briefed him "off the record" that he would not be appointed because the panel considered him to have been too successful for his age. Nigel regarded this remark as very unprofessional, although kindly intended. As a Christian, he did not want to cause waves and decided to leave it to God. Frank, an outsider with an impressive academic record, was duly appointed. Nigel was very disappointed, but he accepted this outcome and vowed to be as helpful as possible. It quickly became evident, however, that Frank had no managerial ability. In fact, his general handling of his colleagues ranged from poor to dreadful. Even more difficult was the fact that he had a very egocentric personality and seemed to thrive on generating new disputes with colleagues on a daily basis. Nigel struggled with this, seeing that he could have done the job so much better and wondering what God was trying to teach him in all of this strife. He struggled hard to avoid conflict, but it was impossible. Frank simply thrived on creating it – he seemed to need to open up a new battlefront with somebody new at least twice a day. Nigel did not want to be seen to be acting out of his own disappointment at not getting the new post. And, to make matters even worse, Frank was a secular humanist who had already made it clear that he had little interest in people of faith. After much thought and prayer, Nigel decided to try to speak to Frank about his many relationship problems with a view to offering some help. Frank was incensed. "Are you trying to suggest that I have a personality problem? Just because people here seem to like you and don't understand my style? Please mind your own business." Nigel was dumbfounded. How could it be part of God's plan to bring this man into his life?

● *David and William – a clash of values.* David was a Christian, but he was also a tough, fair and direct businessman. He had a good track record of taking care of his people. He ran his plastics business very well and was widely recognized as an industry leader, both technologically and commercially. He was always willing to help people, especially with finding employment. This spirit of generosity had sometimes caused him problems. David had hired William, an active lay preacher and church elder – but a man conscious of his rights and rather forthright in his demands for them. In effect, he was not always a user-friendly type of employee. In hindsight, the hire was a marginal call at best. When the company faced severe competition for its European and Far Eastern markets, David had to announce a program of plant closures, restructuring and lay offs. William could not handle this. Although he was not directly affected, he mercilessly criticized David, behind his back, for his unchristian behavior. David found out about this criticism from a friend at a local church and was very angry. He confronted William, "I do not want to have to do this. But if I don't, there will be no company to employ any of us". William took the high moral ground and said, "This action of yours will destroy the Christian witness in this town for the next decade. You should simply resign in protest". David knew that, if he did, the business would fold. The banks would only support him through this difficult time because of his past performance and good stewardship of their money. David was tempted to make sure that William was on the list of those to leave the company – but he considered that would be wrong and likely to be misinterpreted.

● *Alex and Fred – partners in trouble.* Alex and Fred, both Christians, were business partners in an information technology company. They were at college together and during that time pledged that sometime they would start a business together. It would be founded and run on Christian principles, with integrity, honesty, regard for people and so on, yet developed in such a way as to give them a competitive edge in their market place. They kept in touch in the early years of their careers, although one was in Dallas and the other in London. Seven years after graduation they met in New York and, six months later, New Dawn Consulting was formed as a partnership. Their original vision was undiminished. For the first five years, the business prospered and their families grew closer together. Too close, as it happens, because Alex's wife left him to have an affair with Fred's younger brother. The business partners were devastated, but in spite of the raft of mixed emotions this situation caused, they decided to stay in business. This was not easy, and inevitably each took sides in the family problems. But the business relationship did survive – until, that is, Fred discovered that Alex had been producing false invoices in his side of the company in order to inflate the performance of his division. Fred knew that Alex was under great pressure with the children. The divorce had been messy and expensive. Alex had not personally gained from these actions and there was no fraud. But there was deceit, and the basis of trust was broken – perhaps gone forever. Fred wondered how he could raise this topic with Alex without losing a long-standing friend. Conflict seemed inevitable, and at a time when Alex was very vulnerable.

● *Mary – joining a war zone.* Mary was a hospital administrator who had just taken up a post in a busy general hospital. She was forty-five years old, her children had grown up, she had completed a refresher course and was fired up for this job. She was sure that this was what God wanted her to do. After all, there had been stiff competition for the job and she was amazed that she had come through as the favored candidate. The first week was great. Senior and junior colleagues were welcoming and seemed to want to chat about social and work issues. "What a terrific witness opportunity this will be", she thought. But she gradually became aware that there was a serious agenda underlying some of the friendly comments. "Has anyone told you about the complex personal life of the boss?" "My advice is not to trust anyone here – because they will not trust you." "The doctors are the gods here, everyone else is treated like dirt – just watch and you'll see." "You will have to quickly decide whose side you are on here – there are three, by the way!" By the end of the first month, Mary's stress levels were at an all time high. Although she was not in conflict with anyone personally, judging by the whispers in the corridor everyone else seemed to be. "This is a version of the war of the worlds", she told her husband John, "I'm worried about conflict by association". John wasn't a Christian but remembered Mary's conviction that this was the job for her. Rather unhelpfully, he reminded her of that. Mary wondered where to go from here.

Lessons from Proverbs

The Bible is not short on relevant advice concerning conflict. Some of this advice is found in Proverbs, a book that contains many wise words about how people should relate to one another.[11] Although Proverbs is not a business manual, it does contain lots of things that we need to know. What follows here touches on only a few of these pieces of advice. Conflict situations tend to expose attitudes that are normally hidden, and one attitude that is often absent from situations of conflict is a generosity of spirit. Therefore, counsel such as "A generous man will prosper; he who refreshes others will himself be refreshed"[12] is worth listening to. Here, the "refreshing of others" implies behavior that is generous far beyond reason. Such is God's expectation of his followers. We know from experience that conflict and criticism often go together. On occasion, it is our job to bring critical appraisal to different individuals. Before we approach such situations, the Bible encourages us to think carefully and note that "The purposes of a man's heart are deep waters, but a man of understanding draws them out".[13] You may not feel that you are always such a person – and neither do I. The care with which we speak in all situations is the subject of much comment among our peers. "Reckless words pierce like a sword, but the tongue of the wise brings healing."[14] Equally difficult to apply is advice such as, "He who answers before listening – that is his folly and his shame".[15] The challenge for all Christians in situations of conflict is to

> A generous man will prosper; he who refreshes others will himself be refreshed

consider "what is wisdom's way here?". In all of these verses, the responsibility rests on the wise person – the follower of Jesus Christ. After all, God does not command either obedience or wisdom from those around us at work, but he does require us to be wise. In the heat of a moment of conflict or in its aftermath, you might wonder whether this is reasonable. "Does God expect something of me that I can't deliver?" No, but he can deliver. If you're inclined to say, "I just can't take this type of unrealistic advice anywhere near my work situation", I would encourage you to think again. When you say that, you are saying something very serious about the lordship of Christ in your life – which we will now consider.

Conflict – with our owner   I know many Christians who have lost the peace of God in their lives because of their work. You might be among their number. This path to "conflict" (an absence of peace and therefore of harmony with God and his purposes) with the Lord can begin at any number of different points. It may have come, for example, from a promotion too far; from adopting a lifestyle that demands a total commitment to earnings; from drifting into a work-related social environment that drags people away from Christian fellowship; from adopting the values and culture of the workplace in order to survive its rigors; or from a total separation of work and faith because it just makes life too complicated and faith is not considered important in the workplace. It may even have come from being in perpetual conflict with work colleagues, and from just giving up the fight. However it may have happened, many have lost this peace and do not know how to get it back.

Peace is a very full and positive word in the Bible. It involves "wholeness", a state of integrity, harmony and completeness of a person in a community. Salvation through faith in Christ restores this wholeness. Jesus said, "My peace I give to you".[16] This peace was his legacy to his disciples. It's not a legacy locked up in a remote bank vault or lost in a galleon at the bottom of the ocean. Nor can one have it only after complex litigation. What kind of peace was it? Firstly, it was inward and not dependent on outward circumstances. "That's easier said than done in my work", you might say (and I agree). Yet this is what Jesus left us. It can be achieved; and he wants us to have it.

Jesus said, "My peace I give to you"

Secondly, it was linked to his vocation and the single purpose that integrated his life. This, too, is quite a challenge for us. Many of us live complex lives, juggling numerous priorities. The call of God is to integrate co-working with him towards a very clear end. It's very easy to live lives of separate compartments, inviting the Lord into some of them but consciously excluding him from others. We might choose to live that way – but how can that achieve the goal of bringing glory to his name? That's the plan, and he is the master planner. Thirdly, his peace came from obedience to the Father. Our peace will only come this way as well – don't look for peace without obedience.

In the fourteenth century, Petrarch observed that the five great enemies to peace were "greed, ambition, envy, anger and pride". How many of these five vices have strong links to work and money (the product of work) in our contemporary environment? They all have, in some instances – and so Christians find themselves in conflict with their owner – the one that they have pledged to make the Sovereign Lord of their lives. How can we resolve this conflict? There is little doubt that having and sustaining inner peace with God has everything to do with how my will relates to his will and purpose for my life. There is, as C.H. Spurgeon remarked, the need for another conflict to be reinstated in many of our lives. "If you aim to have peace with God, there must be war with Satan."

the five great enemies to peace were "greed, ambition, envy, anger and pride"

There is a further kind of conflict with our owner which is the enemy of peace. This conflict stems from discontentment – with how the world of work has treated us, with our position in it, with the way in which others have fared better in their careers, with feelings of being underpaid, undervalued, passed over and exploited. Because of such feelings some people despise their jobs – a state of mind not conducive to bringing God glory. These very real problems are getting worse as our societies (and, sadly, our churches) become more success oriented. In some ways this leaves a whole group of Christians "in dispute" with the Lord, with some bearing a grudge against God. I have great sympathy for such people. At the spiritual level, these issues can only be addressed by finding God's answer to a simple question, "Why am I here, Lord?". The biblical answers lie in being reassured about who we really work for and in having confidence in his choice of employment location for us. "Whatever you do, work at it with all your heart, as working for the Lord, not for men".[17] To answer such questions we also need to lift our sights from this life to the next, "I consider that our present sufferings are not worth comparing with the glory that will be revealed in us".[18] But, for some, such comfort is not real enough to deal with present hurts. The Bible is clear that, for better or worse, our faith develops within our place of work. How, for example, can a verse like, "Since we live by the Spirit, let us keep in step with the Spirit"[19] possibly exclude the major part of our lives that is taken up with secular work? As Ian Clark summarizes so well, "the disciple of Christ knows his own personal weaknesses but realises that, so long as he keeps in Christ's company, nothing is impossible".[20]

In order to resolve conflicts with our owner we need to receive and accept his plan for our lives. Although this process can be difficult, we need to take a longer-term perspective on our lives than we will get from our peers. This poem by Alex Muir, one of my early Christian mentors, has spoken volumes to me over many years. To the best of my knowledge it has never before been published.

The Plan

When I stand at the Judgement Seat of Christ
And he shows his plan for me:
The plan of my life as it might have been
Had he had his way; and I see
How I blocked him here and checked him there
And would not yield to his will;
Will there be grief in my Saviour's eyes
Grief though he loves me still?

He would have me rich but I stand there poor,
Stripped of all but his grace:
As memory runs like a haunted thing
Down the years it cannot retrace:
Then my desolate heart will well nigh break

With the tears that I cannot shed,
I'll cover my face with my empty hands
And bow my uncovered head.

Lord of the years that are left to me
I yield them to thy hand:
Take me, melt me, mould me
To the pattern thou hast planned.

☑ **ACTION:** If you are "in conflict" with the owner, try to trace when and why it started. In diagnosing your situation, you might want to think about the symptoms in areas such as time allocation, determining priorities, following God's advice (see the section on Proverbs, above), your relationship with God, your attitude towards your work and so on. Spend some time seeking and confirming that you and the Lord are working to the same plan in your work. To do this properly you might need to briefly write out your career plan and then ask what signals you believe God has given to either confirm or change it. It is unlikely that you will find peace as long as your plan diverges from that of the Lord!

Challenge No5

There are many difficult challenges in this chapter. Reflect on the different but closely connected sets of relationships in your work and on God's view of the world in which you live your Christian life. (This will also help you to prepare for the next chapter on discipleship at work.)

1 How does the love of God show in your life at work?

2 Christians have a ministry of reconciliation. Is it one that you practice at work?

3 One of the fruits of the Spirit is kindness. How have you displayed kindness (or how might you have done so) in a situation of conflict?

4 You trust in God. But do people who work with you trust you?

Further reading

Anderson, Neil T., and Rich Miller, *Getting Anger under Control* (Eugene, OR: Harvest House, 2002).

Curran, Peter, *All the Hours God Sends?: Practical and Biblical Help in Meeting the Demands of Work* (Leicester: IVP, 2000).

Kendall, R.T., *Total Forgiveness* (London: Hodder & Stoughton, 2001).

Zigarelli, Michael A., *Faith at Work: Overcoming the Obstacles of Being Christ-Like in the Workplace* (Chicago: Moody Press, 2000).

Endnotes

1 Rom. 8:7-8.

2 Jn. 17:14.

3 Eph. 2:1-2.

4 2 Tim. 2:4.

5 2 Tim. 4:10.

6 1 Cor. 7:31.

7 1 Jn. 2:16.

8 1 Jn. 5:4.

9 Stott, *Contemporary Christian*, Ch. 6.

10 See, e.g., Mt. 5-7.

11 Michael A. Zigarelli's *Management by Proverbs: Applying Timeless Wisdom in the Workplace* (Chicago: Moody Press, 1999) is a very helpful book that outlines these principles in the managerial context.

12 Prov. 11:25.

13 Prov. 20:5.

14 Prov. 12:18.

15 Prov. 18:13.

16 Jn. 14:27.

17 Col. 3:23.

18 Rom. 8:18.

19 Gal. 5:25.

20 Ian Clark, *Reservoir of Power* (Glasgow: Pickering & Inglis, 1980), 'Foreword', p. 2.

6
Discipleship at Work

"This is to my Father's glory, that you bear much fruit, showing yourselves to be my disciples."
(Jn. 15:8)

Outline   Jesus asks us to follow him and learn from him. Because the Lord blesses us with his Spirit in our hearts, he accompanies us to work every day. But can those with whom we work see enough – or indeed any – evidence of that? This chapter investigates just how effective our discipleship can be in a work environment, provided that we depend on God every step of the way. After proposing that we do some new thinking about work, this chapter poses three questions and gives lots of biblical answers.

Fresh thinking about my work
First we examine why we need to think in a new way about our work in order to fulfill our calling as disciples, then we recall the objectives set for us and marvel at the way in which Peter introduces the example of Jesus.

What are the people I work with learning about Christ from me?
Our colleagues learn from us as we demonstrate our Christian character. We will look at two specific aspects of this character, namely integrity and the ways in which we demonstrate the fruit of the Spirit in our lives at work.

... and how do they learn?
Jesus chose salt, light and seed sowing to illustrate the behavior that he is looking for in our witness at work. We will flesh these out with some real-life applications.

What difference has Jesus made so far in my work?
In the spirit of performance review, this section sets out some very practical evidences of Christian character for each of us to address in self-assessment.

Fresh thinking
about my work

You may regard the heading above as a joke. "I hardly ever stop thinking about my work – that's my problem. I don't want a Christian book telling me that I need to think about it even more." Or you might think, "the only way I can cope with my stressful work is to switch off the moment I walk out of the office door and not think about it until I go back again". While many of us can relate to both of these comments, we will have seen by now that we cannot achieve the Lord's standard of discipleship with these attitudes. Most of us probably do need to think more about our work – but in a different way, to specifically and prayerfully address the questions set out in this chapter. These questions, including "What are people I work with learning about Christ from me?", "And how do they learn it?", "What difference does Jesus make in my behavior at work?", "What do God's people look like at work?", are not popular or easy ones. In the challenging words of Joseph Bayley, "Jesus didn't commit the gospel to an advertising agency; he commissioned disciples".

Most of us probably do need to think more about our work – but in a different way

Having begun our study of practice with some cautionary thoughts on some of the dangers and conflicts associated with work in Chapters 4 and 5, we now consider how Christian discipleship applies to our work. But maybe for some of you that is a step too far – the very idea of taking Christ into your particular work environment is still alien. Or you may think that biblical teaching about discipleship sets out an unattainable model, having more to do with idealism than with reality. Many Christians think that way – and act accordingly. Why? Are we not being taught properly? Are we swayed by social and economic pressures? Do we not really know what work-based ministry looks like? Or is it all too difficult? All of these explanations, and many others besides, are quite possible. Most of us have to work with ill-tempered and short-sighted people at some point and have to be responsible to some very unpleasant and unreasonable bosses. We all struggle in these situations to see past the immediate circumstances and remember that "It is the Lord Christ you are serving".[1] Our point of departure, in light of what we learned in Chapters 1 and 2, is that God wants to go to work with us each and every day. In Chapter 2 we asked, "What's so special to God about my particular work?". We noted that the answers included the following:

- To be a witness
- To be shaped by God
- To show God's love in action
- To bring God glory

If we were able to deliver on these four goals, we would be effective disciples for the Lord in our work situation. We would produce the evidence that lies at the heart of our theme text for this chapter, because we would truly be "showing ourselves to be his disciples". If that is the "what" (and it is), the essence of this chapter is to ask ourselves "how do we achieve this?". That's what we have to think about individually and in greater depth. To be passive or neutral about how we approach work is not an option if it is our intention to truly follow Christ.

To be passive or neutral about how we approach work is not an option if it is our intention to truly follow Christ

A disciple is, as the root of the word indicates, a learner. Any Christian disciple has to want knowledge, to realize that applying it is a lifetime task and to be flexible enough to accept that others may be right and we may be wrong. There is no better place to start than with Peter's explanation of Jesus' example. "To this you were called, because Christ suffered for you, leaving you an example, that you should follow in his steps."[2]

This Greek word for "example" had its origins in primary education. It refers to the lines that teachers drew on wax tablets for children to follow as they wrote. In my case it was a slate in a village school, but I well remember the teacher's lines – largely because I had a problem staying within them. I always found the z's difficult, and I did the s's in reverse. What did the teacher do? First she wrote perfect letters at the top of the slate, so that I could copy the correct thing. And then, when I still couldn't do it well, she put her hand over mine to guide me through the shape of the letter. Christ does both of these things in our lives every day – if we let him. But having a superb example without any help can be very discouraging and demoralizing. As I watch the British Open or US Masters golf tournaments, I only want to throw away my own clubs. The professional standard bears no resemblance to the game that I play. I will simply never be able to attain that standard. But the Lord gives both an example and the Spirit to make discipleship at work possible. And we don't have to be perfect to be effective.

What are the people I work with learning about Christ from me? Martyn Lloyd-Jones hit upon a humbling truth when he remarked, "If you try to imitate Christ, the world will praise you; if you become like Christ, the world will hate you!". While there is a sense in which the world welcomes a measure of goodness, people find too much goodness threatening. What does being Christ-like entail? Following are some different aspects of Christian character and behavior.

a) Integrity Let's start by thinking about integrity at work – while recognizing that it is only one aspect of Christian character. According to the dictionary definition, integrity means "adherence to moral principles". It is a word associated with wholeness, uprightness, honesty and purity – all highly desirable evidences of Christ-like behavior. We know, for example, that it is essential to be honest at work with people, with problems, with success and failure, with the acceptance and exercising of authority and so on. If we are not honest, we have no right to be heard by anyone. And, if we are not honest, we rarely are. As Christians, we might even be tempted to hijack the word "integrity" and say that only Christians display this quality. Charles Colson says that "The three most important ingredients in Christian work are integrity, integrity, integrity". But I regularly see people who are far from Christian, or indeed from any faith, practice with a very high degree of integrity. It is therefore necessary to distinguish between the drivers of good behavior at work and integrated Christian practice. They are two very different things – I could comply with the former (and it is vital that I do) without people learning anything very much about Christ from me (see Table 6.1).

TABLE 6.1

Drivers of Christian practice at work

Focus	Content	Scope	Accountability
Law	Statute	Universal	Courts
Secular morality	Codes of conduct	Compliance	Peer groups
Salt and light	Bible	Ambassadors	God

A Christian has to embrace all three of these focus areas at work. And none of us can operate the "on/off" switch in matters of integrity by choosing which moral principles we prefer to embrace or by deferring them on a bad day. Nor can we arrange our affairs by a dual morality, running our personal lives by one set of principles and our business lives by another.

Some Christians try this, and they fail miserably as ambassadors for Christ. Indeed, they succeed only in bringing the cause of Christ into disrepute. Both "peace with God" and witnessing for Christ depend on an integrated life. Table 6.1 tells us that it is important, for example, to comply with the law. But we have to recognize that the law is a moral floor, setting only minimal standards of behavior. Do you remember Jesus' conversation with a certain rich young man? This man was legally compliant in all regards, yet he walked away from the greater and tougher demands of the Lord – to sell his goods and give to the poor.[3] We are to fully adhere to the law as well as to various codes of conduct that surround our work, but this is not enough. Doing that is part of getting us to first base with our fellow workers, and helping to establish our credentials as Christians. Of course, obeying the law is also part of being good citizens as God instructs us to be. Table 6.1 illustrates only one of the distinctively Christian callings, namely to be true ambassadors for the Lord as "salt and light". To fulfill this calling requires a new Spirit-led set of moral principles that are the foundations of Christian integrity. If we live in this way, people will learn a lot about the beauties of Christ through us.

> *Both "peace with God" and witnessing for Christ depend on an integrated life*

A good integrity test for us all comes from the nineteenth-century pen of Josiah Gilbert Holland. In spite of his language, these words are for both men and women.

> *God give us men! A time like this demands*
> *Strong minds, great hearts, true faith and ready hands;*
> *Men whom the lust of office does not kill;*
> *Men who possess opinions and a will;*
> *Men who have honour; men who will not lie*

> ☑ **ACTION:** Do you consistently display Christian integrity at work? Think of specific incidents when your behavior either helped or hindered a work colleague from learning about Christ. What lessons has God been teaching you in this area of integrity? How have you been responding to his prompting?

b) Christian character As we move to the central importance of wider aspects of character, we need to acknowledge that the people we work with may see more of the negative side of Christianity than they do the positive. Christians should adhere to the moral imperatives of the Bible – and so shun lying, adultery, stealing and so on. In so doing, they communicate a message to their peers. But can anyone I work with see positive evidence of the graces of the Spirit in my life? Without them, they will see little of Christ – since they are his virtues. A gardener cannot manufacture fruit – it only comes from the life that is in the plants – a life that the gardener does not initiate. The nature of each plant determines the fruit that it bears – apple trees don't produce strawberries. Each fruit also contains the seed for still more fruit. Christians produce fruit only by the Spirit – hence the great Pauline injunction, "Since we live by the Spirit, let us keep in step with the Spirit".[4] The Bible clearly sets out the characteristics that God wants to see in our lives.[5] The difficulty comes in applying these to the work situation. Their presence, or absence, will determine what those I work with learn about Christ. Although Table 6.2 cannot possibly be exhaustive, it illustrates what is expected of us in this area. Reflect on the illustrations below and how they apply to your conduct at work. Although this is unlikely to be an easy exercise for any of us, we need to remember that the Lord is always there to forgive us and to help us to change.

TABLE 6.2

The fruit of the Spirit in work

● *Love*. Divine love is the root of all the other fruits. Love cannot thrive where there is hatred, bitterness over an injustice or hostility over a lost promotion. Love cannot exist when you treat people ruthlessly, in the politics of the office, in the midst of jealousies over career advancement, when employers or employees are not respected. Loving is at least as demanding an obligation in the workplace as in the rest of life – if not much more so at times.

● *Joy*. The Christian's inward peace and sufficiency should not be affected by outward circumstances – but it often is. Joy doesn't sit well with cynicism, with constant complaining about my job, with my reputation for being negative about everything and everybody. Nor is it easy to show joy when work is not creative or fulfilling, or when boredom and uncertainty are its main ingredients.

● *Peace*. Sourced in God alone, this peace is often not visible in the midst of tension and stress at work. It implies a community of people in right relationships with one another and with God. This is not common in a work environment, but it is what the Christian works for and actively seeks to contribute to. The Christian needs a sense of peace that he is working where God wants him to be. The Christian is to show evidence of inner peace in worrying situations and in times of contentment, as well as through mood swings – none of which is easy.

● *Patience*. A courageous endurance that does not quit, we need to show patience towards God, towards people and towards ourselves. We show it towards God when we want something or someone changed and work is full of inconveniences. We show patience with people when anger, bad temper, spiteful behavior and retaliation would be the easy way. We show it to ourselves when we fail in our witness and report slow progress in producing these other graces.

● *Kindness*. The divine kindness out of which God acts towards human beings is often lost at work due to the formality of organizational structures and reporting lines, aloofness and the process of figuring out how to show it and not appear weak. Preoccupation with our own affairs can stop us from displaying kindness. Sometimes we use the excuse that difficult colleagues would not understand it, or that we are rebuffed when we try to be kind. Kindness is often costly and inconvenient to put into practice – yet it is one of the hallmarks of God's people.

● *Goodness*. We are expected to be good and to do good – since goodness is love in action. For this goodness to have a positive impact, our motives must be pure and we must avoid hypocrisy, boasting and dishonesty at all times. Goodness and integrity are closely linked. We should not be afraid of having a reputation for doing good – it can be a vital witness to, and product of, personal faith.

● *Faithfulness*. This includes the qualities of loyalty, reliability and dependability – all of which are highly valued in most work contexts. They are characteristics that often make even timid disciples stand out because of the sheer quality of their performance. This is an area in which the Lord looks for excellence from us – and in displaying faithfulness we bring glory to him. But such faithfulness can also lead to willing workers being overloaded and promoted beyond their own comfort level.

● *Gentleness*. Often translated "meekness", gentleness involves the right use of power and authority, or power under control. This is unlikely to feature in many modern training manuals where self-assertiveness, focus and aggression are at a premium. Gentleness requires us to avoid throwing our weight around, misusing authority and insisting on our own rights unnecessarily.

● *Self-control*. This is the application of discipline whose aim is fitness for service. Years of Christian witness at work can be destroyed in a momentary loss of self-control – whether in a business meeting, in a heated argument or at an office party. Exercising self-control requires self-restraint in all things, including in working relations with the opposite sex, alcohol, addiction to work, ambitions and language.

It's difficult to think of anything more radical and counter to the prevailing work culture than the contents of Table 6.2. You might say, "The behavior implied here is from another world, and it's light years from mine". And you would be right. It is a brief for the citizens of heaven – and you are one of them as a disciple of Christ. Or you might think, "Whoever wrote this has no earthly idea about the world of work in the twenty-first century". Well, actually he does – since he is the sovereign Lord of all things. You might protest, "There's no way I could take on this remit – no way!" But as a Christian you already have. So the real question becomes, "Where do you get the power to deliver on it?". It's the work of the Spirit to make us like Christ in character. Only the Spirit can produce the fruit of the Spirit. And it will only be produced if we keep in step with the Spirit. It's a waste of time trying to counterfeit these features – there can be no glory for God by that route. Nor can we pick and choose which of them we will specialize in. They are a package. But we should remember that, with the Lord, failure is not fatal – as the lives of Peter and David demonstrate. Yet we also need to know what success looks like. So if we are to work with and for the Lord, we need to closely examine the example – hence the focus of Table 6.2. Did

Jesus take these attitudes into the carpenter's business at Nazareth? He certainly did. He saw it all first hand in the working life of a small trader, with all the complexities that brought. We must assume that he worked in a highly moral way, achieved excellence and treated people with great respect. He displayed such graces where he was, doing what was his to do. Oswald Chambers is right: "If our spiritual life does not grow where we are, it will grow nowhere". You and I are co-workers with the Lord where we work right now, no matter how good or bad it feels there.[6] Our central task is to portray something of Jesus in that setting. And our character usually speaks much louder than our words.

In making ourselves aware of the awesome nature of the task of displaying Christian character at work, we must not miss the fact that God requires this fruit for a purpose. We display the fruit of the Spirit not so that others can admire it (or us), but so that they will desire it. People around us are looking for a Christian faith that actually works. As Warren Wiersbe perceptively observes, "People around us are starving for love, joy, peace and all the other graces of the Spirit. When they find them in our lives, they know that we have something that they lack."[7] I recently heard a radio commentator say, "It's the God part that's missing in our lives, so we've turned to poor substitutes". One of our roles is to show how to fill that gap. One of the principal ways that we do this is by living out these graces. We attribute them to Jesus Christ, and we want others to do the same. Glorifying the Lord is indeed the driving force – that is the essence of the opportunity – and this in turn is a central part of the answer to our "whose work is it anyway?" question.

☑ **ACTION:** Your first inclination might be to take a break here – to pause, think and pray. Pause to get a new sense of what God wants from you in your work situation; think about the opportunities that the evidence of these graces in our working lives would, or do, create; and pray that you will keep in step with the Spirit to make this possible. Part of this might involve an honest "character check" and some self-assessment on these nine features. On a scale of one to ten, how would you score yourself in terms of how you display each fruit in your working environment? This appraisal will help you to better understand how people are learning about Christ through you – and what it is that they are learning. In the light of all this, list some things you can do to be a more effective witness for Christ in your daily job. George Duncan once said, "The fruit of the Spirit is not excitement or orthodoxy; it is character".

...and how do they learn? We have seen that our workmates are learning (or failing to learn) about Christ through observing our characters – the kind of people we are in a wide variety of circumstances. These include contexts in which there is little other human support and minimum Christian peer pressure. Without living in constant anxiety, we need to recall that these observations are being made all the time, building up a picture of who we truly are. Would we recognize ourselves if we were able to see that picture? More critically, does the Lord recognize it as an example of discipleship in practice? This section explores three of the many biblical pictures that summarize the behavior that the Lord desires from us at work.

Salt and light "You are the salt of the earth. But if the salt loses its saltiness, how can it be made salty again? It is no longer good for anything, except to be thrown out and trampled by men. You are the light of the world. A city on a hill cannot be hidden."[8] These metaphors are both powerful and pointed. They clearly remind us of the responsibilities that Christians have in all dimensions of their lives. In Jesus' time, salt was an important substance that purified, preserved and gave flavor – by becoming an integral part of whatever it was applied to – yet it also kept its distinctiveness. In the right amount and in the right recipe, salt is a very effective ingredient – even in these health conscious days. But salt can be painful in wounds, and it is bad news for growing most plants. God does not want us to live low-sodium lives at work – sparingly bringing this essential ingredient to our workplace or leaving the salt in our kitchen cupboard back home. On the contrary, our workplaces need Christians who are wholeheartedly involved and who bring a wholesome contribution. Bringing the values and virtues of the kingdom and the qualities of the Christ to work is often profoundly difficult. When do we need to do this? Almost constantly! Our Christian character shows, for example, when we bring a different view to decision making and choices. It shows in the reconciliation of fractured relationships, in countering the evil that surrounds us and in bringing the Christian standard to bear on a multitude of situations. Sometimes we need to speak up when keeping a low profile might seem like a better, or easier, idea. We need to bring Christian values to tough situations when they are not welcomed or when most other colleagues are priding themselves in being "value-free". At it's best, being "salty" means being, and being known to be, Christian in all things at work. It has everything to do with our individual lifestyle and character. The thrust of this verse is that "you and only you" are the salt of the earth. For disciples this is a primary responsibility. If we renounce this responsibility at work, we damage the cause of the kingdom. The pressures to conform and to comply to other norms of corporate culture, styles of working and to kinds of behavior that are really alien to maintaining "saltiness" increase daily. Only the Spirit can help us both to identify these and to resist them.

Sometimes we need to speak up when keeping a low profile might seem like a better, or easier, idea

Jesus came as the "true light that gives light to every man".[9] As his disciples, we inherit that mantle. This light is not just a matter of passive shining, difficult though that is. Being light involves sharing the good news of the gospel. To give illumination once again requires both good deeds and good words. Work should be a very fertile setting for witness because it is a ground upon which so many things are held in common. Many of the barriers between the church and the world are absent, people face the same drudgeries, tensions, excitements, frustrations and triumphs, and so on. It is the real world for most people. Conversation is often more open as a result – and, often, so are lives. This creates opportunities for listening to personal problems, passing on a relevant Christian book, giving a Christian perspective on contemporary issues and so on. This is not always pain-free, however, because this light often brings unwelcome exposure to both people and situations. In the workplace this light challenges dishonesty and malpractice of all kinds. If Christians do not handle the light with care, they can become the subject of sneering allegations about being the conscience of the organization. Shining without judging is difficult – but essential.

Seed sowing Some aspects of the parable of the farmer sowing his seed have always fascinated and encouraged me and readily apply to the work context.[10] The farmer sowed his seed in a very liberal way. In Jesus' time, the sower threw the seed to the wind as he walked through the field with a seed sack by his side. There was neither time nor inclination to take all the stones away first. The sower simply took the view that a certain proportion would land in good soil. It was not a case of planting the odd seed in regimented rows. At the moment of sowing, no particular attention was paid to the quality of the soil – if it had been, farmers would have saved a lot of money buying seed! At that stage, the receptiveness of the soil was a second-order problem, and seed landed in all types of soil. The sower would carefully choose, however, the month and day to launch his season. So there was a plan behind what appeared to be random. It is also important to note that not all the seed that Jesus himself sowed bore evident fruit. Much of the soil was very hostile – but he continued to sow. In this parable, three out of the four soil types were unfruitful. In our work contexts, our daily task is to sow seed – doing so liberally, accepting that we cannot predict the yield or the response of the soil. The one thing we do know is who is the Lord of the harvest. With all of this in mind we should be careful of how we think about seed sowing. "It's just not worth it in this factory, workshop, office, play group – nobody here has any interest in God." "This is a heathen environment, no seed could penetrate this soil – it's more like concrete than a garden." "I've been sowing for years and I'm still waiting for my first sign of life. The only effect so far is that I have been consistently by-passed for promotion." These are all understandable human reactions, but it's always worth sowing all the same.

> Sometimes you have to wait a long time for any evidence of a harvest

Sometimes you have to wait a long time for any evidence of a harvest. But it's important to remember that it's not our harvest – it belongs to the Lord. A few years ago, at the twenty-fifth anniversary of a church plant that my wife and I were involved with in our mid-twenties, I witnessed the truth of that. A couple with two children spoke to me. The lady said that she was sorry she had never been able to meet me again to say that she had come to Christ after a talk I gave at a youth club over twenty-five years ago. This was wonderful news and very encouraging – but the Lord whose crop she was part of had known about it for years! One of the ways that I sow seed is by giving away Christian books. These can only be "sown" with prayer and a willingness to follow up as required. They are not, however, sown on the basis that I can calculate the returns. Some are welcomed, others are not well-received and some are not even acknowledged. But that is of no consequence.

Personal application Each Christian has to work out his own way of putting these lessons into practice. For many years, my approach has been to immediately tell people I am going to work with that I am a follower of Jesus Christ, including at job interviews. In my case, this involves a lot of people in many different organizations. I try to do this in the first meeting with everybody, regardless of standing or status. It's not a preach-in: it's just the first step. I do it for both their interests and for mine. It puts both of us on notice as to what to expect from each other – although the other person often does not know what to expect, and I have to help them. It also establishes a platform for my future behavior and trying to be salt and light. And their reaction? Well, it varies enormously. In most cases it's polite indifference, in some cases it raises questions and (quite often) it draws out a secret disciple or a lapsed one. People largely take the "if that's your thing, that's fine" approach – treating it as of little more significance than stamp collecting or hill walking. Building on that platform has had many fascinating consequences. For example, at my own university the Christian Union prepares an annual list for new students,

I had signaled that I was willing to talk about Christ

citing the members of staff who are prepared to be known as followers of Christ. At one time, I was the only person out of a large faculty making this public declaration – although there were other believers. Because of this I had many conversations with students for whom my name being on the list opened the door. I had signaled that I was willing to talk about Christ. Sometimes that's all it takes at work – an initial, and early, signal. In quite a different context, I once had an earnest conversation with the chairman of a public company of which I was a director. He was deeply puzzled by the newfound faith and "enormous enthusiasm" that his daughter now had for the Lord Jesus. He was a very sophisticated, cultured and learned man, and he simply could not understand where this came from – having been a casual, ritualistic church visitor all his life. I gave him a copy of one of the late David Watson's books. At the next board meeting, he astonished me (and everybody else) by introducing the agenda as follows: "Neil gave me an interesting book about Christian faith. Over the holiday break, I've read every word of it – I wish I could accept all of this; but he is going to tell us about his own faith before we start this morning". Opportunity sometimes knocks at unexpected times! I did this, of course – even though the cynics around the table thought that the chairman had lost the plot.

☑ **ACTION:** One way or another, you will have kept a record of your working life. It might be in the form of a biography or a C.V. Others might have less need for such formality because you are a homemaker, self-employed, in a family business, retired, suffering ill-health and so on. You might want to either look at your record or think about what you would put into it if you had to write it down. What does it show? What does it not show? Many aspects of our lives are not, of course, captured in such a document. Think about the spiritual dimension of your life and service, and ask what is likely to appear on God's version of your biography. Remember that all aspects of your work are of interest to him.

Having done all of that, contemplate the truth of this remark by Craig Blomberg, "Christians can live with integrity under virtually any economic system, but they can only do so by using their personal resources in accordance with scriptural principles".[11]

What difference has Jesus made so far in my work?

A central part of our normal work environment is the assessment of our progress. Few of us are exempt from someone measuring our performance and giving us feedback on how we are doing. In my own case, I am subject to many different ways of being measured – depending on the contribution that I am required to make. They range from the views of shareholders on company profits to the outcomes of research review processes in academic life to the evaluation of government agencies in terms of value for the spending of public money. The Bible clearly teaches that God will someday review each of us, based on an overview of our lives. Meanwhile, he is able by his Spirit to give us an ongoing evaluation of our discipleship. And he often does this through the Bible, teaching, pastoral advice, Christian books and so on. How do you react to these periodic reviews and private feedback? As the saying goes, "reputation is what men think you are; character is what God knows you are".

In the spirit of review, what follows is a method for self-assessment. In everyday life, Christian character at work shows itself in many different ways. Only a few of these manifestations are listed below, but they are the ones by which many people assess who we really are, and they are very practical. As you read through, ask yourself what progress you are making at work as a Christian in the following areas.

● *In your conversation.* What do you talk about other than work activities? How do the language you use and the way you speak reflect the fruit of the Spirit? Do your conversations convey what matters in your life? How much does God feature in what you say?

● *In your attitude to people.* Do you consistently show care, consideration and humanity? Does your behavior show evidence of love being translated into daily practice with all your fellow workers – independent of their relative standing and status in any organization?

● *In your attitude to work.* Is your attitude clearly in step with the Spirit in terms of ambition, cynicism, contentment, work-life balance, honesty and so on? Is your attitude clearly different from that of other, non-Christian, colleagues?

● *In your morality.* Have you established and expressed Christian standards? Have you observed them consistently?

● *In your overall behavior.* Would anyone that you work with, or for, be surprised to find that you were a follower of Jesus Christ? Sometimes people cannot hear a Christian word we say because of who we are.

Challenge No6

In reviewing the challenges contained in this chapter, we turn first of all to the succinct and direct challenge in our theme text.

1 In our working lives, to what extent do we "show ourselves to be his disciples"? Would those we work with be able to give evidence to that effect?

2 If you feel that such a question applies, what specifically is it that stops work being a mission field in your case?

3 Do you have a reputation for Christian integrity where you work? If you do, pray that the Lord will preserve it. If you don't, ask God to give you the strength to change your life – and be prepared to accept the consequences. Discipleship doesn't come cheap.

4 Attachment to the church without daily discipleship has been described as the husk without the kernel. Do you need to work to nurture the inner disciplines beneath the husk? What are some specific ways that you can show more of the fruit of the Spirit at work?

5 Apply the truth of William Barclay's remark about the disciple to your own situation. "Every single piece of work he produces must be good enough to show God." Is it?

Further reading

Anders, Max, *The Good Life: Living with Meaning in a 'Never Enough' World* (Dallas: Word, 1993).

Chewning, Richard C., John W. Eby and Shirley J. Roels, *Business through the Eyes of Faith* (Leicester: IVP, 1992).

Hughes, Selwyn, *Christ-Empowered Living* (Nashville, TN: Broadman & Holman, 2001).

Thwaites, James, T*he Church Beyond the Congregation* (Carlisle: Paternoster, 1999).

Endnotes

1 Col. 3:24.

2 1 Pet. 2:21.

3 Mk. 10:17-22.

4 Gal. 5:25.

5 For an excellent exposition of these characteristics, see Stephen F. Winward, *Fruit of the Spirit* (Leicester: IVP, 1981).

6 Christian character is a crucial part of Bible teaching. Should you wish to follow up other New Testament references, they include Eph. 4:2-3; Col. 3:12-14; 1 Tim. 6:11; Jas. 3:17-18; 2 Pet. 1:5-9.

7 Warren W. Wiersbe, *Galatians: Be Free* (Amersham-on-the-Hill: Scripture Press, 1986), p. 136.

8 Mt. 5:13-14.

9 Jn. 1:9.

10 Mk. 4:3-9, 13-20.

11 Craig L. Blomberg, *Interpreting the Parables* (Leicester: IVP, 1990), p. 309.

7
Working at the Moral Edge

"Since we have these promises, dear friends, let us purify ourselves from everything that contaminates body and spirit, perfecting holiness out of reverence for God." (2 Cor. 7:1)

Outline The material in this chapter follows very closely on the discussions concerning Christian behavior in Chapter 6. We focus here on one very visible and telling aspect of discipleship at work – namely the ethics by which we live. This chapter explores the way that our ethics affect the many decisions and moral judgments that we make each day in the workplace. It is often in this specific area that our Christian witness either stands or falls.

Why think of a moral edge?

Christians rarely have an ethical base that perfectly mirrors that of their employer. Christians find that peer groups and the observed lifestyle choices of their peers, job-related organizations of which they are members and the standards and practices of their industry or profession can all be sources of pressure to compromise biblical principles. Three Christian approaches to ethical behavior include followers, wanderers and dissenters.

What should a Christian focus on?

We turn here to look at God's character and foundational biblical principles to determine the Christian's focus. This section examines five important behavioral evidences – speaking the truth; treating people with respect; obedience to an alert conscience; behaving justly; and practicing Christian love – and some of the ways in which we are deflected from living these out.

Everyday moral choices at work
In order to recognize how ethical choices quite literally surround us at work, this section examines four brief cases in the contexts of diverse careers.

What does divine power in action look like?
This final section explores the amazing, effective power that God has made available to us so that we can take these tasks on and be ambassadors for Christ.

Why think of a moral edge?   "As the sailor locates his position on the sea by "shooting" the sun, so we may get our moral bearings by looking at God." This quotation from A.W. Tozer sets us on the right course for this chapter – in which we are much more interested in practical and personal Christian living than in debating moral philosophy. If our character perfectly mirrored that described in Chapter 6, and we effectively displayed the fruit of the Spirit, it would naturally follow that we put into practice the ethics that Jesus taught. That would constitute God-honoring ethical behavior. The Bible is neither a business nor an organizational manual. It does not spell out a specific code of ethical practice for every work situation – it does much more than that. As we read the Bible, God, through the power of the Holy Spirit, seeks to transform our hearts and therefore our characters. By so doing it equips us for every moral dilemma – and we all face many in our work. We are Christian from the inside out – so obeying the external laws and rules, important though they are, is only an outward manifestation of the conviction and power within us. Think about Peter's words to people going through some really tough persecution. "But in your hearts set apart Christ as Lord. Always be prepared to give an answer to everyone who asks you to give the reason for the hope that you have. But do this with gentleness and respect".[1] Indeed, we do need to be able to both practice and explain our Christian ethics. They are a product of a change of heart, a consequence of the reorientation of the center of our lives. Oswald Chambers expresses this idea very well: "Morality is not only correct conduct on the outside, but correct thinking within where only God can see". Your work colleagues have many different ideas about what is right and wrong; they may even query whether "right" and "wrong" are valid concepts or whether there is such a thing as right and wrong. People who work together do not usually swap lists of each other's moral principles or post them on the intranet or in the house newsletter. Neither do we spend much time discussing such principles as abstract concepts. Often people will only know what our ethical standards are by observing our actions and behavior. People know that we are Christians by the way we act. And some may already have formed their own opinion as to whose payroll we are on – and perhaps we would not be proud of their conclusions.

Figure 7.1 TWO VIEWS OF ETHICS AT WORK

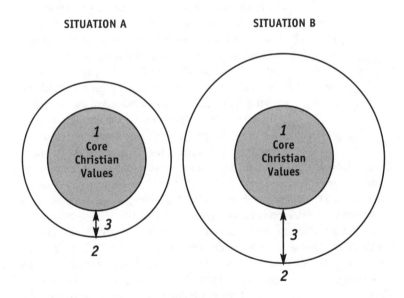

Notes:

2 – The value framework of our work environment

3 – The moral gap

The metaphor of the "moral edge" in this chapter illustrates a simple but vital point about Christian ethics in our work. Figure 7.1 will help us. The outer circle represents the overall mix of views of right and wrong in your place of work. These come from many sources – from the personal views of individuals, some of which may be derived from a faith; the application of professional standards and codes of conduct; the rules of the organization; the laws of the country and so on. The inner and smaller circle represents the ethics that Christians try to apply to work, based on their changed character. This circle is smaller because it has much clearer principles and should have fewer "gray areas". It does, of course, include laws, rules and codes. And it's based on what God commands for his people. It's smaller for another set of reasons as well. For many people, conversations about right and wrong often begin, "It all depends on the situation ...". A Christian would expect to have fewer of these conversations. Indeed, he may be unpopular because he sees things from a "black and white" perspective. Living out and explaining this counter-cultural set of values is a struggle, and we often fail. But John gives us a telling biblical picture in his reference to disciples "walking in the light". This is one illustration of the content of that inner circle. "But if we walk in the light, as he is in the light, we have fellowship with one another, and the blood of Jesus, his Son, purifies us from every sin."[2] Not one of us is without sin, and we are all capable of going over the moral edge. Therefore Figure 7.1 depicts two circles with a gap between them. Many Christians testify to the fact that this gap is growing in many different work environments. As it grows, the Christian is likely to be more out of step with the moral climate in which he works. The diagram distinguishes between work environments "A" and "B". In "A", the Christian may be in an environment where his values are understood and even welcomed – for example in a Christian-led company or ministry, or in an organization with high moral standards (from whatever source). Here the "gap" still exists, but it is much narrower. The gap still exists because of factors outside the organization and because of the fallenness of all the actors, but the Christian working in this environment spends less time and energy worrying about falling off "the moral edge". The work environment represented by "B" portrays a situation with which more of us will be familiar. Most Christians are very aware of some sort of gap – if you are

Not one of us is without sin, and we are all capable of going over the moral edge

not, perhaps you might want to think more deeply about it. Some observe the gap growing in their present employment and feel increasingly uncomfortable as a result.

What happens when we allow ourselves to be drawn towards, or we fall off, the moral edge in our work? Among the many stresses associated with "bridging the gap" are the following types of push and pull pressures. These pressures are evident at all ages and phases of working life, although those in the earlier and more vulnerable stages of a career may feel them more strongly.

Peer group pressure You may be asked questions such as the following. "Everybody who went on last month's training course exaggerated their expense claims – why should you be different?" "We are all covering up on the time sheets for Jean, you know that her mother is ill – what's your problem?" "Including a porn show at one Christmas party wouldn't do you any harm. Surely your beliefs are not that shaky?"

> We are all covering up on the time sheets for Jean, you know that her mother is ill – what's your problem?

Lifestyle pressure These personal pressures flow from observed peer group lifestyles. You may, for example, feel additional pressure from your spouse: "I don't want to be burdened by hearing about these moral problems you have at work – why can't you just ignore them? Everybody else seems to. After all, you're well paid and we need the money". Or you may find yourself thinking, "I am surrounded by dishonesty and corruption. My witness is a waste of time – but I will never get another job as good as this. I am trapped."

Organizational pressure "The kind of people we need here have to have that extra spark of creativity in all things – including creativity with the truth at times." "You may well find that the demands made by your customer on a night out go way beyond what you are happy with – but just remember that the customer is king in this organization." "Fine, you have your principles – as long as you don't put them before the company. I didn't hire you because of your principles."

Industry and professional pressures "I'm not sure that I can be a criminal lawyer and a Christian – I've almost lost a sense of what is true and what is false, given the people that I deal with all the time." "I'm selling insurance and savings products, and my salary is not related to what is best for my client but to what my best commission is. Sure it's a matter of judgment, but I'm struggling with my conscience." "Everybody cheats and cuts corners in the building industry, so forget your principles and get on with the job. All this stuff about health and safety is just bureaucracy."

The net effect of all of these examples – and they represent only the tip of a very large iceberg – is that Christians are pushed towards, and sometimes over, the boundaries of their principles into the norms that others are quite relaxed about. Fortunately, most of us do not face these issues every day. But every job involves some of these pressures and choices – somewhere, sometime. They usually steal up on you when you are least prepared, and they often center on everyday routine matters. We would do well to refer to our theme text from 2 Corinthians and remember that our behavior is to be "out of reverence for God".

As we examine the possible responses to these pressures more closely, it is important to remember also that God knows our hearts and has a unique insight into our motives at all times. The words of Thomas Aquinas both challenge and encourage us: "A man's heart is right when he wills what God wills". At the same time, we acknowledge that we exercise choice, we respond in different ways to pressures in the workplace, and at times we lose touch with where our hearts should be. On the basis of the picture in Figure 7.1, Christians can approach ethical behavior at work in any one of the following ways.

> *A man's heart is right when he wills what God wills*

● *A follower*. He finds out about, and sticks to, his core beliefs – as taught in the Bible and as practiced by Jesus. He makes no claim that this is easy, but he knows that it is right. He is regularly tested and his dependency on Christ is often pushed to even greater limits.

● *A wanderer*. He lives as close to the edge of his beliefs as he thinks he can. He presumes, mistakenly, that no one really notices or cares very much. He is very willing to experiment with what he really believes. He has occasional spasms of conscience.

● *A dissenter*. He likes the idea of a gap and is usually found in it, because there he can speak loftily about his moral principles and do what he likes in practice. He is rarely troubled by his position, because he has succeeded in separating work and faith. He once had an active conscience, but it's now gone. He buried it long ago.

☑️ **ACTION:** Before we proceed any further with this subject, try placing yourself into one of the three categories above (or another, if you find you need a new category). Before you choose one, try to think of up to six choices or decisions that you have made at work over recent months that posed moral dilemmas (you weren't sure whether they were right or wrong). Were the decisions you made in character with being a follower of Jesus Christ? How have others responded to them? Have these choices helped or hindered your witness? Have you experienced any of the four types of moral pressure discussed above? If so, which ones have you handled best?

What should a Christian focus on?

We cannot, in this section, cover the entire canon of Christian ethics at work. Nor can we explore all the complexities associated with their application. Rather, we will focus on a few of the very telling moral dimensions of Christian character that require our detailed and consistent attention. Without these, our witness will be inhibited and our co-working with God will be blemished. It is important to note first, however, that it is possible to be highly moral without reference to Christianity or any other faith. Many atheists and humanists have a keen sense of right and wrong, are passionate about justice and show great care for people. And there is considerable overlap between Christian ethics and other human-centered ethical systems. Simply exhibiting behavior that is ethical is not enough. As Daniel Wilson wisely said, "Morality does not make a Christian, yet no man can be a Christian without it". The Christian practice of ethics has to come from a God who is at the center of our lives and who has transformed our outlook on the world of work (as well as our outlook on all other aspects of our lives). When we stray from our central relationship with Christ, our morality goes off-track soon after. The Christian's morality is built on a loving and obedient relationship with God. That relationship is its sole foundation. Paul's words are worth remembering, "Be imitators of God, therefore, as dearly loved children and live a life of love, just as Christ loved us and gave himself up for us as a fragrant offering and sacrifice to God".[3] How, then, do we keep ourselves prepared for life in a moral maze at work?

● *Remember God' s character.* The three intertwined divine characteristics of holiness, justice and love have a direct bearing on all Christian ethical behavior. In determining our conduct, we can't choose between them. Although these qualities are not always easy to translate into a world of flawed humanity, they remain the bedrock for Christians. Jim Packer's words are stark: "We live in the age of God-shrinkers. For many, God is no more than a smudge".[4] We should make sure that Christians are not among them!

● *Remember the foundational principles.* The Ten Commandments are very relevant here, since God requires us to obey them. Unless we exercise this essential obedience, we will have no foundation for living a moral life.[5] The commandments ask us to build two basic things into our lives – reverence for God and respect for humankind. This two-directional focus is the very essence of Christianity. We dare not separate them, tempted though we may be by the pressures of work. Only by God's grace can we show the necessary respect for humankind in all types of work situations while at the same time regarding our work as part of our worship of God.

Only by God's grace can we show the necessary respect for humankind in all types of work situations

● *Remember Jesus' teaching.* It is very evident in the Sermon on the Mount, especially, that what Jesus was teaching was radical and far from the accepted norms. Nothing changes, does it? It has always been possible to claim to be "a great Bible student" and yet live in a way that is far removed from what we read in the pages of the New Testament. As has been wisely said, Christianity is obedience.

Our only effective weapons for spiritual warfare at work are the empowerment of the Spirit and prayerfully reminding ourselves daily of these three building blocks. Only with this divine help will be able to exhibit Christ-honoring moral behavior. For our peers at work, this really is where the rubber hits the road. It's based on the following type of evidence that people form a view of the characters of Christians in the workplace. The five marks of Christian behavior cited below are all foundational.

Speaking the truth "The LORD detests lying lips, but he delights in men who are truthful".[6] These are very strong words, and we have to take them seriously. Honesty is perhaps the one personal characteristic that is most valued in both employers and employees. We are given many serious biblical warnings on this topic, including, "No-one who practices deceit will dwell in my house; no-one who speaks falsely will stand in my presence".[7] Not all Christians are honest, although many think they are and go into denial about what they say at times. It is not common that someone admits to lying. But evidence of lying is seriously damaging to the Christian cause. As Matthew Henry wrote many years ago, "There is nothing more offensive to God than deceit in commerce". This is a salutary thought for us all to absorb!

There is nothing more offensive to God than deceit in commerce

Treating people with respect This quality is rooted in the love of God. Moreover, Christians believe that, in spite of sin, all men and women retain the image of God. Treating everyone with that in mind is a moral imperative. But it can be very difficult to put this into practice with some people in whose behavior it is almost impossible to see that residual spiritual core. I am at times appalled by how some Christians treat others with whom they work – and it's noticed. This behavior sometimes stems from arrogance and pride, which are impossible to justify on the basis of either God's love or his holiness.

Obedience to an alert conscience The area of conscience can be a dangerous one. On occasions we can find that our consciences are clear when they have no right to be. They have been deadened by the company we keep and by our own lack of faithfulness. Take some aspects of holiness at work, for example. One important consequence of following Christ is purity in conversations, intentions and in our attitudes to sexual immorality. Reflect on the directness of Jesus' comments to his disciples when he told them that it would be better to be blind or lame than to adopt lower ethical standards.[8] You might call that unreasonable, but he made his point with conviction. And we name him as Lord of our lives.

Behaving justly The complex issue of rights and duties is always an area of potential tension in the workplace. A Christian has to try to make decisions in an impartial way, free of conflicts of interest. The Christian needs a balanced approach, for example, to gathering evidence in a dispute, giving people the right to be heard and behaving with due process. Insisting unreasonably on our own rights can send very conflicting messages to our peers or employers. Applied without love, justice can be cold and dispassionate. So, for example, Christians making decisions in areas such as the implementation of alcohol policies and health-related absences from work need special wisdom.

Practicing Christian love Many of us would want to argue that this is the pivotal point of Christian ethics – not least because the Bible itself regards it as such.[9] In terms of relative ranking, Jesus expressed it in these terms. "'Love the Lord your God with all your heart and with all your soul and with all your mind.' This is the first and greatest commandment. And the second is like it: 'Love your neighbor as yourself'".[10] That instruction does not leave much room for doubt. Love has a great deal to do with relationships, creating as it does bonds between people. Many Christians blanch at the thought of having to translate love into the marketplace. Yet we cannot conduct our business and professional lives without effective relationships. But what ingredients distinguish Christian love? These include an ability to empathize with others, whatever their problem; not trying to settle scores or retaliate; being willing to go several extra miles with difficult colleagues; and being able to forgive, when that is very challenging.[11] Christian love really is *the* distinguishing mark of Christian life.

"Love the Lord your God with all your heart and with all your soul and with all your mind"

It would be very easy to diminish the weight and force of these principles by rationalizing that it is too difficult and complex to apply them in every situation. This sort of thought process often ends with a shrug of the shoulders – as if such challenges only give us a vision of what should be, but never quite is. Too many discussions about morality with Christians end with "this is all too difficult" types of phrases. But Christians should make every effort to apply these principles to the simple, everyday events at work – where it is only too obvious what the appropriate Christian behavior should be. This practice establishes the habit of focusing on the essentials of Christian ethical behavior. We then lean heavily on God for guidance in the really complex situations. My own problems with applying the Bible come not from the passages that I do not understand, but from those that I understand only too well. Perhaps you have a similar experience. And, ultimately, it is a matter of obedience. As Sinclair Ferguson asserts, "There is no such thing as genuine knowledge of God that does not show itself in obedience to his Word and will".

Alexander Hill, in his excellent book on this subject,[12] discusses three types of "false exits" whereby the biblical standards we have just discussed are diluted or avoided by some elegant (and not so elegant) arguments on the part of Christians in the marketplace. The first such "false exit" is the view that the culture in which the individual works defines what is acceptable – whether at an organizational or country level. So dual morality is born and justified – but the tensions persist, since it is virtually impossible to simply replace Christian morality with that of the prevailing culture. Second is the belief that compliance with the civil law is in itself enough to satisfy the Lord – irrespective of the quality of the legal system or its moral basis. In response to this view, we could safely say that legal compliance is a necessary moral duty for the Christian, but that it does not constitute ethical behavior in and of itself. The third "false exit" concerns the challenging question as to whether Christians are ever justified in lowering their personal moral standards when acting as agents for their employers. Unfortunately we cannot fully develop these crucial issues in this context, but it is important for us to think them through.

☑ **ACTION:** In response to the serious and demanding teaching here, first consider how you are currently displaying the five types of behavior discussed above in your workplace. Think very specifically here. If this review saddens you, ask God how you could change that and take him further into your work environment. Secondly, ask yourself if you are currently taking any "false exits", or versions of them, to avoid the force of biblical teaching on morality at work. If so, what would it take to get you back on to God's moral highway?

Everyday moral choices at work

J.A. Motyer has said, "To the Bible, history is the arena of moral decisions, moral conflicts and moral consequences". Life certainly feels like that. Often when a Christian interacts with others in a work context there is a moral dimension to that interaction. This is not something that should cause either fear or paranoia. Being aware of the moral dimension of our behavior in every aspect of life is a consequence of being ambassadors for Christ. Here are Paul's powerful words, "We are therefore Christ's ambassadors, as though God were making his appeal through us".[13] This is a telling observation – and part of God's appeal is the demonstration of the character of Christ through our ethical behavior. In what follows we will highlight the universality of these "touch points" (points of contact where we make decisions, consciously or unconsciously, about our moral response) for two reasons. First, we need to understand how much we need God in our life at work. Second, we need to think more carefully about the opportunities and threats to Christian witness that surround us. The four job examples below underscore these points.

> *First, we need to understand how much we need God in our life at work*

● *George – Sales executive.* He is in a position of trust, and he is given much scope to do his job as he pleases – provided that his results are in line with the budget. Because George travels extensively, he has to take care as to how he uses his time in hotels and avoid the temptations that come from having spare time and being bored. These might include adjacent nightclubs, excessive alcohol and undesirable hotel videos. In his selling, he needs to be truthful about promises he makes, comparisons of product performance, prices, delivery dates – and avoid the temptations of financial and other kickbacks that prevail in his trade. On the financial side, he needs to take care in calculating expenses and commission payments. His business colleagues are very competitive and there is a strong materialistic culture in his organization. He wants to perform well yet avoid the trap of materialism in his life.

● *Ann – Social worker.* Ann is a pioneer in her profession and operates in a difficult inner city environment. Some of her moral challenges involve making honest and balanced judgments about problem families. She worries about how to see people professionally, yet through Christian eyes. She has some non-Christian colleagues who think that she spends too much time on individual cases making sure that she has it right. They criticize her in case conferences for not being dispassionate enough. High profile and very public cases of professional failure by care workers make her more anxious. Issues of respect for people, a sense of injustice and personal integrity are all high on her agenda – and her compromise list, because sometimes it is easier to go with the flow.

● *Dave – Entrepreneur.* He has always been a car enthusiast. He has bought and sold them since he was at school – before he became a Christian. He is full of energy and ideas, and he knows that he is in an industry with a bad reputation. Among the challenges he faces are determining and communicating the true condition of cars that he sells and their reported mileage, as well as deciding the prices he pays his suppliers and those he charges his customers. Other challenges include his compliance with all the "nuisances" of taxation and accounting, health and safety legislation and employee conditions – things that some of his competitors ignore rather too often. He does regard much of this as "a bit over the top" – and he is tempted to cut corners. "What do these bureaucrats know about business?" is one of his common sayings. He faces challenges on other fronts, too – not least of which is how much time he has to spend with his family. He is great with customers, but he can be rough with his employees – and fortunately he knows it.

● *Norman – Equity salesman.* Norman just loves the cut and thrust of financial markets. It fascinates him intellectually and gives him a real buzz. He is a salesman in the stock-broking side of a major investment bank. Markets are down and business is not going well. Volume trading is needed as a matter of urgency. He is tempted to promote poor, high-risk stocks; to listen to in-house whispers from his colleagues that he is not supposed by law to hear; and to lure clients into trades just for the sake of it. It's a world of rumor and counter-rumor – where truth is not at a premium. Of course, it's all wrapped up in the formality of compliance and procedures. He recognizes the moral hypocrisy of many of his colleagues who are appalled by high-profile corporate scandals yet who display personal avarice on a grand scale daily. He has to try to stand free from it, or get out from under it.

> ☑ **ACTION:** While you might want to reflect on these four brief insights into the careers of others, try doing this sort of analysis on your own current job as well. Accepting that there are many "touch points" in each of our working lives, try to identify the ones that most frequently give you ethical problems at the present time. Which ones seem to offer you the greatest opportunities for witness?

We all feel at times that our working lives are like living in a moral maze. There are many ways ahead, but one ethical principle seems to clash with another as we try to discern the best path to take. I find that these clashes are sharpest when I am involved in something that could lead to the cause of Christ being held in disrepute. Although a situation may not have resulted from any wrongdoing on my part, it may lead to guilt by association. I can recall many such instances in my career, including the following three examples. At one point I had to deal with a colleague who had a serious, but largely hidden, alcohol abuse problem. Love told me to be all I could to this man and steer him to professional assistance. But fairness to others, poor performance and absenteeism led me ultimately to have to ask for his resignation. Although I would have preferred the route of love to prevail, I had to implement the latter one. In another context, where I was representing investors in a company, there was a persistent refusal by the executive directors to implement board policy after it had been agreed. It was a family company. Truth and openness had been abandoned, and relationships between family members were very strained. After many vain attempts to try to get good governance in the company, I had to insist on financial backing for this business being removed, to the risk of the jobs involved. I was torn between making the business decision with the most integrity and respect for the people concerned – the outcome was unpleasant for the management team concerned. In a third case, the police telephoned me. They wanted to meet to privately discuss a business unit whose parent company I advised. They approached me because they knew I was a Christian. It emerged that the police had uncovered a major criminal fraud involving the management, of which the owners had no knowledge. The police informed me about this and left me to decide what to do. Honesty and integrity required that I tell the (incredulous) owners immediately – although I could foresee the huge public scandal, the closure of the business unit, employment loss, damage to innocent people and potential prison sentences. All of these consequences did come to pass in the ensuing months. In this context, it was clear that I had no choice. It is virtually impossible to pursue the ethics of the Savior without bearing scars, and I have many of them myself. And so I lead you to the only possible way of living effectively at the moral edge – the power of God.

What does divine power in action look like? When the word that we translate as "energy" occurs in the New Testament, it always implies effective action – namely, action that is strong and powerful and that leads to the desired and intended result. This word is used, for example, to describe the miraculous power that worked in the miracles of Jesus[14] and to the evidence of his power in the church. "Does God give you his Spirit and work miracles among you because you observe the law, or because you believe what you heard?"[15] But the word also refers to the power that works in the life of the Christian – and this usage is of special importance for this chapter and this whole book. Paul writes in the following very encouraging terms. "Now to him who is able to do immeasurably more than all we ask or imagine, according to his power that is at work within us, to him be glory in the church and in Christ Jesus throughout all generations, for ever and ever! Amen!"[16] It is that inner power alone that makes Christian life at all possible – not least in our testing work environments. As Joni Eareckson Tada once remarked, "The weaker we feel, the harder we lean on God. And the harder we lean, the stronger we grow." The Bible makes it clear that this effective power of God shows up in many ways. It is evident in the resurrection, in the church, in the defeat of sin – but it also shows up through love, in our evangelizing and in personal morality. It's part of our daily challenge. Aren't you glad that we are not expected to do any of this in our own strength? The question at the beginning of this section is, "What does divine power in action look like?" And the answer? It looks like you and me! At least that was the designer's intention.

Challenge No7

Would you honestly say that you are living out the designer's intention through your ethical behavior at work?

1 How would you respond to the view that there are no general principles for Christian morality and that to imply there are merely leads to legalistic Christianity?

2 Think about ways in which Paul's message to Christian leaders might apply to your position where you work. "He must also have a good reputation with outsiders, so that he will not fall into disgrace and into the devil's trap."[17]

3 Are Christian morals for Christians or for all others where you work?

4 Think and pray about the ethical impression that you have left with all those with whom you have interacted in your last working week.

5 Reflect on the saying that God does not call the prepared, but he prepares those he calls.

Further reading

Barclay, William, *Christian Ethics for Today* (San Francisco: Harper & Row, 1971).

Ryken, Leland, *Work and Leisure in Christian Perspective* (Portland, OR: Multnomah Press, 1987).

Vardy, Peter, and Paul Grosch, *The Puzzle of Ethics* (London: HarperCollins, 1994).

Williams, Oliver, and John Houck, *Full Value: Cases in Christian Ethics* (San Francisco: Harper & Row, 1978).

Endnotes

1 1 Pet. 3:15-16.

2 1 Jn. 1:7.

3 Eph. 5:1-2.

4 Packer, *Rediscovering Holiness*, pp. 68-69.

5 One very thoughtful treatment of the Ten Commandments is to be found in

William Barclay, *The Plain Man's Guide to Ethics* (Glasgow: Fontana, 1973).

6 Prov. 12:22.

7 Ps. 101:7.

8 Mt. 18:7-9.

9 1 Cor. 13:13.

10 Mt. 22:37-38.

11 Mt. 5:38-42.

12 Alexander Hill, *Just Business: Christian Ethics for the Market Place* (Downers Grove, IL: IVP, 1997). See in particular Part 2, on 'False Exits'.

13 2 Cor. 5:20.

14 Mt. 14:2.

15 Gal. 3:5.

16 Eph. 3:20-21; see also Col. 1:9-14, esp. v. 11.

17 1 Tim. 3:7.

8
Living through a Work Crisis

"For I know the plans I have for you, declares the Lord, plans to prosper you and not to harm you, plans to give you a hope and a future." (Jer. 29:11)

Outline   All of us, at some point, face circumstances that take on crisis proportions, and these can often be work related. When we are in the midst of these crises they disrupt our lives in a most unwelcome way, even though we may subsequently see them in a different light. We will explore a number of these crises in this, the final chapter in Part 3 on our practice at work. After examining the feeling of exclusion associated with such situations, the core of the chapter considers four groups of work-related crises. Throughout the chapter, experiences from the lives of different Christians illustrate and help to clarify the discussion.

Working for God – but feeling excluded
This introductory section considers the type of events that can lead us to disconnect our lives from some of the foundational principles discussed in Chapters 1 to 3. These events can be divided into four general categories.

What do I do when the world of work bypasses me?
Here we look sensitively and practically at selected cases within each of the categories – getting into work; staying in work; leaving work involuntarily; retiring from work. The aim is for all of us to try to better understand these experiences and therefore to make us more able to assist and support friends and colleagues living through such circumstances.

Learning from Elijah's crisis
Elijah's work crisis highlights some widely applicable principles. His journey through the stages of being in the grip of fear, in the eye of God, in a state of ignorance and in the path of God has much to teach us all.

Working for God – but feeling excluded Many different events and situations make it very difficult for individuals to give the correct Christian answer to the question, "Whose work is it anyway?" because they have short or long-term difficulties in relating to, and connecting with, the world of work. People experience these dilemmas for a whole host of reasons. Sometimes these difficulties arise out of the mistaken belief that we can only be co-workers with God if we are in paid employment. Nothing could be further from the truth. We need to approach this topic with sensitivity and humility, since many of us have had no direct personal experience of these circumstances, and indeed few of us will even be aware of them all. But many of us will have observed their effects and witnessed their devastating impact on other people – including on Christians. For example, although I have never been laid off, I have worked with and tried to help many who have been. Many of us have not experienced the trauma of persistent illness that excludes people of all ages from the gainful employment that they so much desire – but some of us have witnessed its effects by caring for those who have. Allan Chambers said that "Crises refine life. In them you discover what you are". This process of discovery is often a painful and private one. I have used the word "crises" – decisive moments or turning points – as the collective noun for the topics covered. In reality, crises are often characterized by intense stress, extremity, trouble and disaster – so it's hard to describe them with a single word. For clarity, we will divide work-related crises into four general categories. The groups are quite diverse and include a variety of life experiences – not all of which will be covered in detail in this chapter. But many Christians face each kind of situation below.

TABLE 8.1 CRISES CONNECTED WITH WORK

● *Getting into work.* Finding employment can be a problem for many different people – for those whose upbringing and family circumstances have led to them being socially excluded, an exclusion which is often extended by a limited education; for those who are highly trained at school or college but can find no suitable employment following that training; for temporary workers seeking permanent posts; for those wanting to re-enter paid employment after a lengthy absence; for the long-term unemployed and, in many cases, for those who are physically or mentally disadvantaged.

● *Staying in work*. Similarly, it is difficult for many people to sustain employment. Those with recurring and debilitating health problems or with outdated skills, people who have reached a level where, for various reasons, the career routes ahead are all blocked, as well as those in organizations where there is extreme pressure to reduce numbers employed due to changes in technology, ownership or markets, all experience this difficulty.

● *Leaving work involuntarily*. People at all ages and stages in their working lives, and for various reasons, experience lay offs. Many of them go on to suffer short or long-term unemployment thereafter.

● *Retiring from work*. While some people leave work at the contractually specified age, others leave earlier, or by agreement due to reorganization, mergers and takeovers, or ill-health and so on.

A fifth category, *Prospering as a Christian at work*, is not included in Table 8.1 because, although this situation also has crisis dimensions for many people, the book as a whole addresses this issue. There are several reasons for including a chapter focusing on crisis. The primary reason is to affirm that the work of Christians in all of these situations matters to God and that work for God and being employed are not necessarily linked. The second reason is to remind those of us who are engrossed in our own employment that Christians in these situations need both counseling and pastoral care. And, thirdly, each one of us could find ourselves in a similar situation someday – and some forward thinking about how we might react would be well worth our time.

The same basic principles that we saw in Chapters 1 to 3 apply in these crisis situations, because they are for all Christians at all times. But such crises often produce conditions that make it difficult for a Christian to make sense of the world of work. Because most of our peers assume that employment is a synonym for work, being without regular employment often results in a profound feeling of being excluded. Telling a Christian who finds himself in any of the four categories in Table 8.1 that he is still in God's employment can be interpreted as trite. "Easy to say when it's not you that finds it so difficult to get a permanent job. I have now been on short-term contracts for 15 years." "Can you possibly explain to me why I am unemployed three years after graduation? I was confident that I chose the course God wanted me to take." "I've been forced to retire at age fifty, and I have no idea what to do with the rest of my life – my primary reason for living for the past 30 years is now gone." "I was out of the labor market for 12 years while I was bringing up my family – all the re-entry training has so far come to nothing." These are just a few typical responses from wounded and grieving Christian people. In such situations, a huge spiritual effort is sometimes needed to feel fulfilled through the tasks currently open to them; to have a sense of continuing to serve both humankind and God; and to maintain their calling (using John Stott's phrase) "to make (the Lord) visible, intelligible and desirable". Bitterness, disillusionment and distressed personal circumstances can all be enemies of that calling. Conversely, a positive attitude in such crises can be a powerful witness. The Bible is full of examples of career uncertainties and perplexing development paths in which the outcomes were not obvious to the passive observer. Think of Ruth and Naomi as refugees in need of basic income; of Moses with many career switches and breaks, and his final role being the product of long-term development and much retraining; or of Daniel and Joseph, who both had fulfilling and challenging jobs but would rather have had them back home. Generations of Christians living with uncertainty of all kinds have clung to the promise in the theme text. "'For I know the plans I have for you,' declares the LORD, 'plans to prosper you and not to harm you, plans to give you hope and a future.'"[1] This promise is reassuring, robust and refreshing. We need to be thankful that God is concerned with every detail of our lives and remember, as D.L. Moody said, "God never made a promise that was too good to be true".

☑ **ACTION:** Look again at Table 8.1, taking different perspectives on it. For example, do you find your own particular situation there? You probably know Christians in some of these categories. Consider what help and advice you might offer to them. Whatever your relationship to the world of work, think carefully about how this poem by Annie Johnson Flint applies to you.

Christ has no hands but our hands
To do his work today;
He has no feet but our feet

> To lead men in his way;
> He has no tongues but our tongues
> To tell men how he died;
> He has no help but our help
> To bring them to his side.

What do I do when the world of work bypasses me?

There is no easy answer to this question, so I won't try to give one. But, for the reasons mentioned above, let's look at a few of the many situations faced by Christians within each of the four groups in Table 8.1 and look to the Bible for advice that will benefit all of us – whether our experience of these difficulties is direct or indirect. Over the past 30 years, I have spent time discussing career changes with many different people – not as an expert, but as a concerned person. I have done this in part because I am interested in career paths, and in part because I am a Christian. Most of these people have not been Christians, and so these discussions have resulted in many witness opportunities. For Christians in these positions, the challenge is to maintain a sense of purpose and mission in their lives. While some people show great strength and are able to lean on the Lord throughout such crises, many really struggle. Most of the illustrations that follow are based on real people in real crises within my broad circle of Christian friends over recent years.

Getting into work

The six different people in this category described below all feel excluded from work and cannot find a way to break into it. They suffer because society associates work with success, material wealth and status. People in the first subgroup of this category, however, may lack skills and not have the inclination to acquire them – in part because they have never been encouraged so to do or have no family role models. They may have been nurtured in a culture of dependency on state social provision for any number of reasons. Some are new to the Christian faith and therefore have few role models at home or in the church. It is helpful for those lacking skills to get involved in some form of disciplined activity, even if it is voluntary, and take all the advice and training they can get. These people often do not have a good network of support and contacts and need help to do this – and they may need such help at many different times. Biblically, we are to find and develop God-given aptitudes within his people, be good stewards of what

we will be able to witness to God's transforming power in our own lives

we have, foster order in our lives and establish good relationships, in the context of which we will be able to witness to God's transforming power in our own lives. Cases like this are far from easy. They are often quite frustrating and require a lot of persistence. Dan, for example – a man with many of the above characteristics – once told me that he did not want to work. "People like you get heart attacks from working – there's no way that's going to happen to me!" This attitude was difficult to comprehend and, I suggested to him, not a good starting point for a Christian. But if work continues to pass such people by, cynicism, bitterness and a sense of being rejected – even by other Christians – often follow. Some people are able to overcome such trials and witness to God's transforming power in such circumstances, but most need help to triumph over these struggles.

The next subgroup includes those who are highly trained but cannot find appropriate employment. Maria, for example, had always planned to be a primary school teacher – since her days in Sunday club. Her involvement with primary-age church groups and various camps throughout her teenage years had confirmed this. Everyone who saw her work with small children regarded her as a "natural teacher". She was rather like the Pied Piper, followed by little children. She was convinced, through prayer, that God was calling her to this profession. She passed through college with flying colors but, when she completed her studies, there were 35 students in her graduating class and only four jobs in her locality. Her mother had a severe stress-related illness, and so she was reluctant to move any distance from home. She continued to interview and work voluntarily as a classroom assistant, but two years later she still had no teaching post. By this time she had worked in many temporary and unfulfilling jobs. Maria had moved from disappointment to distress and then to disillusionment as her dreams failed to materialize. There are many people like Maria, and when speaking with them my approach is to ask the Lord to reaffirm his apparent specific direction for their lives – if this is really the Lord's purpose, there will be an opportunity ahead. If they truly feel that this chosen profession is their calling, then they should find work (paid or voluntary) that is as closely related as possible to what they want to do to demonstrate their worth and gain experience. I usually also tell people in this situation that career paths are rarely in straight lines – something that is news to them, and to many others as well. I also encourage them to be flexible about when and how this calling will be realized, on the grounds that they are better to be in the world of work than out of it and that God may not always have exactly the same plan, or method of implementation, as we expect. Part of the process of helping such people is to gently guide them to consider what God is teaching them through this experience.

The most difficult subgroup of those trying to get into work is the long-term unemployed. Yet among this group are many contented Christians who know that their work belongs to the Lord. While some of them would prefer to be earning a living in traditional ways, any number of reasons, including health problems and involvement in long-term care within their families, preclude this. They are willing and committed Christian workers who would put others with apparently greater resources to shame. There are, of course, many others who cannot seem to come to terms with their situation. They show all the classic symptoms: a sense of failure, loss of self-esteem, insecurity, depression and despair – and therefore they often need professional counseling. It is often very difficult for people in these situations to rethink their lives – they often do not have either the energy or flexibility to do that. Although we may not always realize it, Christian ministries of all kinds provide many such people with routes to fulfillment. For example, many contribute in a major way by caring, praying and offering a wide range of practical help within a Christian community. We should support the church in taking a lead in this area and encourage people to take these opportunities – even while waiting for employment. Involvement in ministry to others can provide excellent therapy, and it's a great way to put the Bible into practice. As Paul wrote to the Romans, "Therefore, I urge you, brothers, in view of God's mercy, to offer your bodies as living sacrifices, holy and pleasing to God – which is your spiritual worship".[2] For people in such situations, the link between their work and their worship can so easily be broken simply because there is an aching gap in their lives.

> *It is often very difficult for people in these situations to rethink their lives*

Staying in work   While this section explores some of the subgroups mentioned above in Table 8.1, the heading will also sound all too familiar to many others. Recent years have seen heightened levels of risk and uncertainty about the quantity, quality and duration of work in many countries. Meanwhile, work brings conflict to many, as seen in Chapter 5; while others feel threatened by its complexities and the directions of change, as we saw in Chapter 3. Part of the general work-related anxiety of many Christians is worry about staying in work. Oswald Chambers remarks that "worry is an indication that we think that God cannot look after us". Many of us would have to plead guilty to this. All of us need to learn from Jesus' powerful words. "Look at the birds of the air; they do not sow or reap or store away in barns, and yet your heavenly Father feeds them. Are you not much more valuable than they?"[3] If you are in this state of worry, ask God to remind you of your value to him. Start by looking again at the cross of Christ.

The first subgroup from Table 8.1 that we will explore here consists of those who feel that they have, or are about to, hit a brick wall in their careers. They may feel this way for any number of reasons, including their lack of qualifications, outdated skills, attitudes, discrimination or performance. They feel undervalued and often change jobs regularly to offset one or other of these difficulties. There are many Christians for whom staying in work is a problem, and I have tried to help some of them – with varying degrees of success. People in these situations often know verses like, "I have learned the secret of being content in any and every situation, whether well fed or hungry, whether living in plenty or in want".[4] But they cannot, or will not, apply this verse to their work situation. For whatever reason, they will not be content to accept things as they are. Let me tell you about one of them. Walter had never been that interested in studying. He hated school and had no desire to take the extension classes that his employer demanded. The first seven years of his work in an accountant's practice went reasonably well. He was good with numbers and worked hard. But, now married and in his late twenties, he became more and more irritated by the new and fully qualified recruits being promoted above him. "They know nothing about this business – all theory and no experience. It'll tell in the long run." However he looked at it, he was a partly qualified accountant going nowhere in this office. Rather than do a serious career review, or return to studying,

There are many Christians for whom staying in work is a problem

he decided to stay and be a critic. (A good Christian critic, of course!) By the time he was thirty-five, Walter was so resentful, bitter and twisted that he was bad company, a poor employee and an ineffective witness for Christ. One of the biggest problems in trying to advise such people is to get them to recognize that the real employment problem lies in their attitude; and how it is linked to bringing God glory. Invariably, people in these circumstances exhibit a streak of vigorous denial. If they honestly review their true position before God with some gracious but direct practical help, they can move to another track. Many are not prepared to think in a sufficiently radical way about their employment. The cause of Christ suffers because many Christian people have this "chip on their shoulder" attitude to work. How can people with such attitudes glorify God?

The next subgroup, of those with debilitating health problems, is difficult for different reasons. Many are the heroic achievements of people who struggle to stay in work in such cases. One Christian friend, who worked in the same organization as I did, had suffered from chronic fatigue syndrome for a long time. Jeremy's colleagues were very supportive over an extended period. They shared his workload, covered during his unpredictable absences and were generally very helpful. One day he surprised me by telling me that he felt that, as a Christian, he had to resign because he had not been pulling his weight. He was under no organizational pressure to do so, but he felt the pressure internally. "The problem is", he said, "I can't handle everybody being so nice to me – I'm so grateful to the Lord, but I just have to go away and think about my future in a new way." In spite of my advice to take a career break and maintain his employment links, he did leave and subsequently recovered. I cite this case because I found it profoundly humbling. It showed me how little I really knew about the way people in these situations feel – and how impossible it is to generalize. Another group seriously affected by health problems includes those who have to leave work in order to become full-time carers for close family members. I have one particular Christian friend in that category who left a senior post in industry several years ago to care for his wife. His tender love and gentleness towards his wife in very trying circumstances have demonstrated the love of Christ to all who know them. He may be absent from the world of work, but he is right at the

I can't handle everybody being so nice to me

frontier of the work of Christ. He reminds me of the great truth in the words of A.W. Tozer, "the call of Christ is always a promotion".

Leaving work involuntarily Some Christians tend to think that being laid off and unemployment are the only two work-related problems that concern Christians. We have seen that this is not the case at all, yet there is little doubt that for all concerned such events are very traumatic and arouse a whole series of emotions that can disrupt a Christian's life.[5] The process of coming to terms with being laid off is often a harrowing one. Initial shock is accompanied by loss of self-esteem, status, income, security, friendships, career prospects and so on. Optimism and pessimism, in different measures, often follow thereafter. New opportunities, new beginnings and a belief that the threatened redundancy might not happen are tempered by a loss of a sense of being valued or even of having any value in the current work environment. Feelings of failure, loss of confidence, anger, resignation and mental and physical distress are all part of the process as well. All of this involves much stress, sometimes depression, and a sense of despair. I would never belittle any of this or be critical of Christians or others who are experiencing it. For most people this is a truly dreadful experience. And many have to repeatedly suffer being laid off through no fault of their own.

Having seen people in these circumstances over many years, I have concluded that sympathetic listening is crucial. It is essential to allow time for grieving, to be realistic about the options and to offer help to pursue them. People need to be personally and proactively engaged in the process of coming to terms with the situation and finding a way forward – especially since they often see themselves as victims. Since I am not a counselor, there are many cases that I would not attempt to handle – my own area of expertise is in offering practical help to take the next steps in rebuilding a career. The one thing that we can all do is to encourage those in this situation. And our theme text from Jeremiah is a vital part of that, when it feels that God has no such plan for us. The three examples that follow remind those of us with plenty of work opportunities that we are all capable of giving substantive help in such times of special need.

I have concluded that sympathetic listening is crucial

Donald, a Christian businessman and managing director of his company, was laid off without warning after 25 years of service. Although I did not know him well, he called my office one evening in desperation. "I have to talk with someone away from my family and friends. Someone who will listen, understand and be honest with me." He was a self-starter, but he was totally shocked that this could happen to him. Apart from the usual concerns about his wife and young family, he had one other surprising worry. "I know no one outside my business and have not written a CV for over 25 years." We worked together for some months and he changed direction in his career to good effect.

James was a proud man with some business experience. When his company went into voluntary liquidation, his job went with it – as well as his lifestyle. His health was not good, and his one concern was that his business problems would not sully a lifetime of Christian witness. In this case I was able to give him some practical help with the realization of assets. It was helpful to be able to share with him about the God-given ability to be still and know God (see Chapter 3).

Quite often, I have been able to encourage people who have made false starts in their careers or who have tried in vain to make career changes. Many people are in the wrong jobs with regard to their aptitudes. Not all of them find this out by being laid off, although Douglas was one who did. He was in a cut and thrust commercial environment that did not suit him. A reorganization led to his finance role being terminated. We discussed, prayed and explored options for many months. Given his gentle personality, I encouraged him to actively pursue different directions, including self-employment. After many trying and testing months, he is now happily working in educational administration. There were many times when he needed to get through the uncertainty by clinging on to the Lord – not least in matters of faith. As all of us need to accept, "faith is being sure of what we hope for and certain of what we do not see."[6]

Many people are in the wrong jobs with regard to their aptitudes

Being laid off does not always have negative outcomes, in either the short or long term. There are many stories of longed-for career changes being finally made possible by financial settlements associated with being laid off. Time out for retraining, traveling and radical thinking is often ultimately welcomed. New businesses in some countries result from such initially painful situations. Similarly, there are many Christians who only hear God's call on their lives when they are disrupted from pursuing their own course by a seemingly disastrous event.

Retiring from work

For many Christians, this final category holds no terror or elements of crisis. Happy indeed is their lot in the eyes of many! If the individual is in good health, has taken time to plan purposeful activity and done some prudent financial planning, retirement can be a very desirable state. For some others, the transition associated with retirement is clearly difficult. Many, who have been almost exclusively defined by their work, fear their loss of standing and are sure that they are leaving their employer with so much still to offer. As a consequence, they can suddenly feel old, bored and useless. Many people manage this transition by tapering their activity – as they move, for example, from executive to advisory roles. But such alternatives are not open to everyone. And many retirees also have serious financial concerns. Many Christians approach retirement with anxieties about finding a purpose in life – especially when they are in posts that are very demanding of their time. They often do not have a well-established pattern of Christian service in their lives and wonder if it will be possible to find one. Churches need to take an active interest in promoting resettlement training for retiring Christians. Those who are retiring need to make a renewed effort to distinguish between "work" and "employment". Retirement is only an end to our employment by human beings. For the Christian, there can be no question of retiring from active service – but clearly there are different forms of service open to those in their mature years. The church and many charities are greatly blessed by people who realize all of this. Scores of retired Christian people have an infinite number of skills that can be used for God – from former nurses sorting medicines for shipment to needy countries to the utility engineer who manages a charity warehouse and the retired headmaster who has built and maintains a charity's computer system. I meet many Christians approaching retirement who do not know where to look for such opportunities – and I am happy to point them in the right direction! But not all Christians take a fresh look at their stewardship as they approach this stage in life. And that is to the detriment of the Christian cause. Woodrow Wilson once remarked that, "the princes among us are those who forget themselves and serve mankind". Perhaps that is one of the special challenges of retirement with which God can help us.

Whether we are, or have been, experiencing any of these crises or whether we are encouragers along the way, Paul's words apply to all of us. "There are different ways God works in our lives, but it is the same God who does the work through all of us."[7]

☑ **ACTION:** For some of you, this section may have made difficult reading. The wounds are too fresh and the experience too current, recent or painful. While paid employment may pass you by, God never does. Nor does he exclude you from his work plans. You are on his roster, and a vital part of his resource inventory. Pray for those known to you who are within the groups in Table 8.1. Ask God precisely what you can do to help them – no matter how preoccupied you are with your own working life. The more connected and knowledgeable you are, the more you may be able to help others.

Learning from Elijah's crisis It is impossible to find one single biblical parallel for the diversity of circumstances considered in this chapter. One particular work crisis in the life of the prophet Elijah, however, brings out many relevant principles that apply to crises that so often surround us. The context of 1 Kings 19 is important here. Here was a man with a sterling record of work for God. He had on three occasions been kept alive by a special divine supply of food – by ravens, through a widow's store and by an angel. That he was still alive to experience this crisis was in itself amazing. In his work he had fearlessly rebuked kings, shown great power in prayer and had been honored on several occasions by God. Elijah was an achiever of the best kind. His life had been threatened many, many times. And a further threat from Jezebel sparked off this particular crisis. One perhaps surprising feature of this crisis was that it came soon after one of Elijah's greatest triumphs. God had just vindicated his servant in a test of strength between himself and the prophets of Baal and Asherah. Sometimes we are at our most vulnerable when we think that we are strong.

☑ **ACTION:** Read 1 Kings 19.

● *In the grip of fear.* Fear for his life had sent Elijah running into the desert. He sat down under a tree and prayed that he might die. "'I have had enough, LORD,' he said".[8] Most of us know that feeling – and similar words may have crossed our own lips on occasion. Elijah was in a depressed state of mind and very vulnerable. He had had enough of threat, tension, stress, loneliness and uncertainty. He had had enough of life under a curse of imminent death. This point came after his long experience of God, recent evidence of God's blessing in his work and years of good service – and yet Elijah, like us, had his weak spots. It's easy to say that he should not have been afraid, but he was. Many of us have been there ourselves, even when we know of instruction such as, "Fear God and keep his commandments, for this is the whole duty of man".[9] Elijah's problem was that his fear of a woman temporarily conquered his fear of God. William Gurnall once said, "We fear men so much, because we fear God so little". In this situation, God came to Elijah through an angel with a wake-up call. God gives him food, rest and instruction – the three ingredients that God invariably brings to us when we are in a crisis. Our first priority should be to let go of the fear and find a place where we can hear God again.

We fear men so much, because we fear God so little

● *In the eye of God.* Now some distance away in Horeb, the mountain of God, he spent a night in a cave. The Lord appeared with a startling and penetrating question, "What are you doing here, Elijah?".[10] Of course, God knew very well why Elijah was there – as he knows the background to any parallel situation in our lives. Perhaps the import of the Lord's repeated question was that Elijah was in the wrong place to do his work and in the wrong condition – in terror rather than at peace. But there was more – he was working under false assumptions. He told the Lord that he was alone, the only true follower left in his nation. In his mind, he had known many times that he was never on his own, but his heart said otherwise in this crisis. Sound familiar? There was something else. As he recounted to God just how dire things were in the world around him, he needed to be reminded that he was trying to carry the wrong burdens. The work belonged to the Lord, not to Elijah. So that day the Lord showed himself to Elijah in a fresh way – not in the wind, earthquake or in the fire, but in a gentle whisper. We need to listen carefully – God may be speaking in a gentle whisper. But, however he speaks, listening is essential.

● *In a state of ignorance.* We all have our own view of the world, and Elijah was no exception. His was a dangerous and troublesome view, and one that damaged his spiritual health. He responded to God with these words, "The Israelites have rejected your covenant, broken down your altars, and put your prophets to death with the sword. I am the only one left, and now they are trying to kill me too".[11] Like us, his judgment was suspect under intense pressure. We rarely see with any real clarity in such situations – except with the Lord's help. When he thought that he was on his own, Elijah discounted both God and 7,000 others who had not bowed their knees to false gods. We see Elijah in the agony of self-pity. Into this crisis God spoke. We could paraphrase his words as follows – "Experience my presence again. As you and I meet, and I display my power before you, re-calibrate your life and answer my question again – what are you doing here?". Once more we can see something of great relevance to us here.

● *In the path of God.* "Go out and stand on the mountain in the presence of the LORD, for the LORD is about to pass by."[12] In this particular situation, Elijah was off God's path for his life – something that can easily happen in a crisis. God comes and does three things. He removes Elijah's personal burden of assuming that he was the sole agent of God; he corrects that and the other false assumptions that led him to be in the desert; and he gives him a totally new direction. Elijah received all the much-needed reassurance that only God could provide. He was still part of God's team – in our terms, he was still on the payroll. God had many things for him to do. We find this same man divinely honored, appearing at the transfiguration talking with Moses and Jesus.[13] Elsewhere we are also assured that, "Elijah was a man just like us".[14]

Elijah was a man just like us

✔ ACTION: Give some thought as to how these five principles apply to your own situation. Whether or not you have had a "crisis" with work like those considered in this chapter, you might find a need to re-calibrate your life to God's power again as part of knowing the answer to the question, "Whose work is it anyway?". Indeed, as you have read the story of Elijah, you might feel that you are in some sort of desert, well off God's path, and in need of redirection.

Challenge No8

As you ask God for help to sustain you or a Christian friend through such a crisis, think about the following points.

1 How would you describe your current awareness of God's plan for you? In what ways has that awareness changed through present or past crises? There may be both positive and negative elements in your response – but keep in mind God's positive intent, as illustrated in the theme text from Jeremiah.

2 What have the various crises in your working life, whether great or small, taught you about how your work matters to God?

3 P.T. Forsyth said, "You must live with people to know their problems and live with God in order to solve them". How can you apply this principle to your own situation?

Further reading

Cymbala, Jim, *Fresh Faith* (Grand Rapids: Zondervan, 1999).

Hybels, Bill, *Making Life Work* (Leicester: IVP, 1999).

White, John, *The Fight: A Practical Handbook of Christian Living* (Leicester: IVP, 1977).

Yancey, Philip, *Seeing in the Dark: Faith in Times of Doubt* (London: Marshall Pickering, 1988).

Endnotes

1 Jer. 29:11.

2 Rom. 12:1.

3 Mt. 6:26.

4 Phil. 4:12.

5 This is a subject on which there is much good Christian literature. See, for example, Peter Curran, *Handling Redundancy* (Grove Ethical Studies 99; Cambridge: Grove Books, 1995). There is also a large volume of secular literature for those with a further interest in this area. See, for example, Michael Argyle, *The Social Psychology of Work* (London: Penguin, 2nd edn, 1989).

6 Heb. 11:1.

7 1 Cor. 12:6 (NLT).

8 1 Kgs. 19:4.

9 Ecc. 12:13.

10 1 Kgs. 19:9.

11 1 Kgs. 19:10.

12 1 Kgs. 19:11.

13 Mt. 17:3.

14 Jas. 5:17.

PART FOUR

PROGRESSING IN OUR WORK WITH GOD

9
Working in Line with God's Plan

"Jesus said, 'Go home to your own people. Tell them your story – what the Master did, how he had mercy on you.'" (Mk. 5:19, The Message)

Outline   These final two chapters are all about making progress in our work with God at our side – working together towards joint goals and empowered by his Spirit. Making progress in any journey depends on our point of departure, and earlier chapters have guided each of us to better understand where we are starting from. In this chapter we ask three questions, learn about being on God's payroll and explore a case study from Paul's experience.

Do I understand my call and its consequences?
After determining that we are approaching this question with the right attitude, we investigate what it means to be on God's payroll. Then we explore the importance of telling our own stories after going through a checklist about Christian testimony.

Do I create and take my opportunities?
Having considered our own approach to witnessing, we see that we can learn a lot from the example of Paul, who seized the opportunity with which he was presented in Athens.

How much progress I am making?
We find both reassurance and challenge in assessing our own progress, acknowledging that we need God's answers to our own nagging questions about our work and faith.

Do I understand my call and its consequences? As we begin to consider whether our work is within God's plan, it may be helpful to pause for further reflection. What you get out of this exercise depends on the attitude that you bring to it. First of all, are you convinced that it is right to view your work as a part of God's plan? That is certainly the way he sees it. Secondly, if your work is "outside his plan", because you pursue it purely for your own ends, do you want to change this? And are you ready to pay the costs and face the consequences, as well as to receive the peace and the blessings? As you think about this, consider these astonishing words spoken by David Livingstone (the pioneering nineteenth-century Scottish medical missionary) about his life. "I never made a sacrifice. We ought not to talk of sacrifice when we remember the great sacrifice that He made who left his Father's throne on high to give Himself for us." Unless we catch something of that spirit, we will arrive at the wrong answer to our central question, "Whose work is it anyway?" As we consider how our approach to work fits into God's plan, this chapter follows a simple, logical sequence paralleling the four basic stages in our relationship with God.

● *We hear God's call.* And in hearing we believe, and then we have a "story" to tell the world around us.

● *We follow God's purpose.* When we are open to his direction, we ask for his plan to be shown to us, and the power to implement it.

● *We look for opportunities.* We constantly ask God to guide us to individuals with whom we can share our faith and to circumstances in which we can show our faith in action, always praying for his strength and wisdom to make the most of these opportunities.

● *We pray about our progress.* We ask that all we do will be to God's glory, in his time and to his standards.

The Bible teaches that God calls men and women to work with him

The Bible teaches that God calls men and women to work with him.[1] A working definition of a Christian is someone who has responded to God's call – initially to repent and believe, and then to worship and serve. But we can be guilty of wanting to accept the privileges of that calling while we ignore the responsibilities that it entails – including the call to serve God in, and through, our work. We need to have discernment in order to hear God's call, and he often has to call many, many times before we hear him. In order to respond, we also have to have the courage to take risks. Why is it that we are often prepared to take risks with our health, careers or even our lives by taking part in hazardous activities of various kinds, yet we are not prepared to go in faith with God's plan for our work? Christians will sometimes say, "I will risk my reputation if I am too up-front about my faith at work. What if I fail? Where would that leave my credibility?". Or they may say, "I may not progress in my place of employment the way I should if I show too much of some of God's qualities. People don't understand these things today". The first quote, at least, purports to come out of a godly motivation. But the truth is that God is sovereign, and he will take us through any such failures if we are truly working for him. The second quote is sad, but it is a sentiment that many Christians often tacitly display. Either way, in the wise words of Erwin Lutzer, "God calls us to live a life we cannot live, so that we must depend on him for supernatural ability. We are called to do the impossible, to live beyond our natural ability". Unless we start there, we will get nowhere.

Throughout this book we have used the metaphor of being on God's payroll – an accessible, yet challenging, way of looking at our working relationship with the Lord. As we turn now to think about it a little more deeply, we must have confidence that God is the world's best possible employer.

Lessons from God's payroll

I'm on a payroll, because somebody hired me. My employers thought that I was worth recruiting, and they saw my potential even when I didn't see it myself. They accepted the responsibility to mentor, develop and train me for tasks initially beyond my capability. My employers understand that people need to be encouraged and supported in order to reach their full potential in their jobs. Some of the things that they ask me to do really stretch me, and I'm not always as conscious as I should be that my boss knows that I feel stretched. I have discovered that I thrive in this "no blame" culture, in which this heavenly employer picks me up, dusts me off and keeps me going. There is no hierarchy in this business – all of us report directly to the top. Access is instant and assured. And nobody measures worth by money. There are millions of others in this great enterprise. It's the original family business, and all the employees are held together in a bond of love. Nobody gets fired – but some employees seem to take long sabbaticals away from the front line of his work. Members of this corporate family come from every cultural group on the planet. Most have never met, yet when they do meet they instantly know each other. Sound incredible? Yes, it does. And you and I are on God's payroll, solely through his divine initiative. We all got here by responding to a call. Part of the joy of being part of this great enterprise is working together towards a common goal and recruiting others. All of those on his payroll sing a song of celebration and attribution to Jesus Christ our Lord. It scans the whole of history and finds only one person worthy of praise:

"And they sang a new song: 'You are worthy to take the scroll and to open the seals, because you were slain, and with your blood you purchased men for God from every tribe and language and people and nation. You have made them to be a kingdom and priests to serve our God, and they will reign on the earth.'"[2]

Everyone on this payroll keeps a record of their experience somewhere in their hearts. Each person has his or her own story. You have yours, and I have mine.

A story worth telling The above theme text from Mark, especially as it is translated in *The Message*, is a powerful lesson from the deranged, disturbed and then restored man from the region of the Gerasenes. He cried out to Jesus in desperation from his home among the tombs. His life was then transformed. He knew it, and so did everybody else who met him. There was no doubt about it. He was immediately commissioned to go and tell. So are we. Working as part of God's plan often involves going "home" to where we are known – to the places where we live and work, to the people who know us, warts and all. God calls us to live and to tell our unique story. All Christians have a story, but some are not absorbed or excited enough by it to want to tell it. Many think that their story is simply a modest one and of no great consequence to anyone. Some of us may have forgotten just how much of God's mercy was involved in our rescue – and how much is still involved in keeping us on track. Others have never thought long enough about their experience to compose their story. If our lives do not tell the same story as our words, telling the story is a waste of time. Helen Keller was once asked if she could think of anything worse than being blind, "Yes," she replied, "to be able to see, but to have no vision". There are few things worse than telling a story that does not match the life. Those who call themselves Christians signify by this very name that they have a wonderful story to tell of God's grace in their lives. But not all Christians tell this story in the context of their work. That's why I wrote this book.

I am a fan of both biography and autobiography – mainly of those relating to the lives of major historical and political figures. There are some great Christian books of this genre, too, that have inspired generations of Jesus' followers. The Bible itself is full of life stories. I am often amazed at the appetite that people have for ghostwritten accounts of some of the most prominent figures in contemporary life – whether in art, culture, sport or politics. In some ways their popularity is indicative of a desire to share in some of the glamor and excitement of celebrity experiences – often because the readers have a lack of purpose in their own lives. Some of these celebrity autobiographies contain a high degree of fantasy, display worrying levels of personal obsession, give insight to inconsequential lives and do not present good role models. Because we are not rich and famous and do not live wildly exciting lives, we may feel that our personal Christian story is not important. This is not God's opinion – and we should remember that. Each one of us is part of the great weight of evidence to the power of the gospel. We need to remember, too, that it is personal testimony that initially attracts many converts to Christianity to explore the faith.

As we have seen, we cannot be co-workers with God if our character is devoid of any of his features. The family of God has to display the family likeness. These godly characteristics, and the way we apply them to everyday situations, add up to our testimony as Christians – namely, the extent to which we demonstrate that Christianity works in our lives. The Christian author Robert Cook was correct when he

we cannot be co-workers with God if our character is devoid of any of his features

observed, "Witnessing is not an effort, it is an overspill". So, in order to work together to God's plan, we need to ask what is spilling over from our lives. Every Christian has a testimony. As you go through the following checklist, consider what your testimony looks like.

● *Who knows that I am a follower of Jesus Christ?* We need to ask this question in several spheres, and your (honest) answer might be different in each. These spheres include: home and family; the neighborhood; the workplace; the broader realms of influence into which work takes you. Many Christians do not want their profession of faith to be known in all of these circles. I've heard few good explanations for this silence, and the Bible is clear that God hasn't heard any. If you have kept such a silence in one or more spheres of your life, I encourage you to think about this afresh, in light of what we have learned thus far. Sadly, I have come across several situations in which work colleagues were astonished to find out that people they had worked with for years were actually Christians. In a studied and calculated way, they had managed to avoid making that explicitly known – by missing opportunities to witness, by not exhibiting Christian character and even by denying the existence of their Christian commitment and activities. This sort of behavior will take a bit of explaining to the Lord at the judgment seat. There is no hiding from the truth that everybody has to know.

There is no hiding from the truth that everybody has to know

● *What do they know?* Those who know that you are a Christian will either know a little or a great deal. This depends to some extent on how closely you work with a person, especially in a large organization. At one extreme, our peers may observe our different lifestyle without understanding why we live this way – and plenty of people have alternative lifestyles for entirely different reasons. "Difference" in itself, therefore, is not enough. It is only through establishing good relationships with our peers that we can both show and explain what it is to be Christian. Many, of course, will not be interested in knowing more or, indeed, knowing anything at all. I am constantly challenged by this and regularly ask myself, "After years of working with me, how often have my colleagues seen a signpost pointing them to Christ?". "Are the people I work with better informed or more misinformed about Christ by knowing me?" You might want to ask yourself similar questions.

● *What are the consequences of their knowing?* There are many such consequences for us, living as Christians. People will look for godly qualities of character and standards of behavior in us and will regard us as a resource in times of need. We need to be prepared to apply Peter's advice, "Always be prepared to give an answer to everyone who asks you to give the reason for the hope that you have".[3] (If you don't have a ready answer, think afresh about your "reasons".) We do, of course, have to ask ourselves a rather pointed question, namely: "Am I prepared for these consequences?". Sadly, some Christians are not – so they live as spiritual hermits, running for cover whenever they are required to represent Christ. Some do this out of fear, anxious that they might not be able to help with appropriate advice or concerned about their scant Bible knowledge. Such people need every ounce of help, prayer and encouragement that we can give them. Others, alas, live this way because standing up for Christ might diminish their standing, status or authority in their job. The latter are often self-assured and confident people in every other regard. For some reason, it is identifying with the Christ of the cross that seems to bring them offense. None of this is what God intended, and we can only imagine the sorrow that it brings him.

● *What happens when they know?* Ultimately, this is in God's hands. But as Paul wrote concerning the witness of slaves in a Christian community "... so that in every way they will make the teaching about God our Savior attractive".[4] This is the result of Christian witness at its best – people want to have what we have. This is the substance of what we considered in Chapter 6, and the essence of all that underpinned Chapters 1-3. If our testimony brings glory to the Lord, then we are ready to move ahead in his plans. If it does not, there will be little salt and light associated with our work lives. There is great truth (and challenge) in the saying that every Christian occupies some kind of pulpit, and preaches some kind of sermon, every day.

☑ **ACTION:** These truths are very challenging. As you consider the above four questions about your present witness to the power of Christ, be quite specific about how they apply to your present work situation – whatever it is. With James, we are taking a careful look in the biblical mirror here.[5] There are several ways to regard this biblical mirror with reference to our reputation at work – the cornerstone upon which we build our witness.

Never look at it. What it shows is too painful and embarrassing. Far too many Christians do this – and they rarely read the Bible. The other danger is thinking that it doesn't tell you much. There is no looking here, because it is assumed not to add value. The Bible is discarded as being immaterial – even to Christian lives.

Give it a casual glance. As we do when rushing to an urgent appointment, both the looking and the learning are only superficial. I call this "the 5 a.m. look" – the attention my mirror gets as I leave to catch a red-eye flight heading for a distant city.

Study what it shows. Wanting to really think through the consequences, you relegate this to whenever you have a spare moment. This is the "I must get around to it sometime" look. Such moments rarely come without a crisis.

Point to the reflections. We do this in the belief that this teaching is for someone else – because they need it much more than you do. Here we give ourselves little more than "observer status". This is the critic's look, distinguished by its own myopia.

Look, think and take remedial action. This is the only truly biblical reaction to the two-edged sword that is God's word. This is what the Lord wants. It is the only look that is consistent with his Lordship over our lives.

Which of these best describes the time you spend in front of the biblical mirror? And what do you plan to do about it?

Do I create and take my opportunities? I have never met a Christian who thinks that he has always been faithful in both creating and seizing opportunities for witness and service at work. I have, however, met some people with a rare talent for engaging in conversation and winning the confidence of others, who are able to create openings that many of us would never see. Equally, I have known some outstanding individuals whose personal quality of character just radiated Christ, yet who were men and women of few words. Many faithful

Christians have a sense of guilt about the extent to which they are able to speak about God to their work colleagues. We need to begin by recognizing our diversity and accepting that the Creator knows about this. But we do also need to distinguish between our relative share of interpersonal skills (which differ dramatically) and our God-given ability to emulate Christ by the power of the Spirit. So as we try to answer this question, "Do I create and take my opportunities?", reflect back to Chapter 6 on discipleship at work. How can we create opportunities? You might be inclined to reply that we simply can't – that only the Spirit can stir the spiritual interests of others. To a large degree that is true, but we need to remember that he may use our example to do some of the stirring! The one thing that we are all empowered to do is to display the beauties of Christ in our workplace. There are no biblical grounds for saying that each and every human being is not capable of this by God's Spirit. Who could ignore such behavior where you work? Would that sort of behavior not, in and of itself, create a wealth of opportunities? Is our behavior not therefore the best place to start?

Most Christians have a lot to learn about understanding their non-Christian work colleagues. We need to pray that God will give us such insight. The following considerations contribute towards the creation of opportunities:[6]

Our colleagues at times sense barriers between us and them, and some of that division is of our making. Some of this comes from having different lifestyles and priorities, but some of it results from our tendency to be judgmental.

Jesus spent time engaging with people, breaking down barriers. The ruling religious elite of the day consistently criticized him for this – but he never stopped doing it.

For a variety of justified and unjustified reasons, some people have very negative attitudes towards Christianity. Some have baggage from their own pasts, and so do we. Whatever else we do, our care, passion and enthusiasm for both God and our colleagues have to be clear.

People need to trust us first, and that takes time – as does building up cumulative evidence of trustworthiness. There is no substitute for the power of example. We have to show people that Christianity relates to real issues in life like loneliness, fear and anxiety.

Many of us need to learn to be silent where necessary, and patience is essential. If we show Christ to people, opportunities will come.

After a while, a diverse torrent of needs often pours out of people – even reserved people. We have to take their needs seriously. Their expectation is that we can help in some way – because our lives have implicitly shown that we are part of God's help team. And so we are.

People often don't have a lot of time to listen. We need to practice summarizing the gospel in few words – perhaps using a verse, parable or personal experience to demonstrate the key principles.

We should be confident that our colleagues need God – although they often do not understand that. Blaise Pascal said that there is a "God-shaped gap" within each of us. This often shows in forms of dissatisfaction with life that create opportunities for witness.

In recognizing our need to understand our colleagues, let's not forget the prior need to understand our own faith – making sure that we have a firm grasp of the fundamentals. How else can we move from building bridges to winning converts? With these observations about opportunity in mind let's examine a specific case about seizing opportunities.

The case of Paul in Athens Only you can identify all the opportunities open to you in your place of work, and some further and important biblical principles may help you in this task. During Paul's visit to Athens, he was able to witness to a whole city. The principles for witnessing to our peers in a work situation are the same. Athens, a cultured city with many idols, is not all that dissimilar from the environment in which many of us work. Such a context combines elegance with weakness; intellectual wealth with poverty; security with fear of the future. We find Paul walking through the city with a very observant eye – looking, assessing, searching for opportunities. Similarly, we need to pray that God would help us to be alert and keen observers. As we reflect on this incident, we will see that there are a series of events, attitudes and observations that collectively characterize Paul's seizing of this opportunity for the Lord.

✔ **ACTION:** Read Acts 17:16-34.

● *A distressed servant.* What was upsetting Paul? "While Paul was waiting for them [Silas and Timothy] in Athens, he was greatly distressed to see that the city was full of idols."[7] Paul was provoked, vexed and stirred by what surrounded him. Both the atmosphere and the people disturbed him. Unless we have the same attitude about those with whom we work and unless we feel the love of Christ constraining us, we will not be able to do God's work effectively. Athens was an impressive city. Its architectural splendor was legendary and its cultural attainments renowned. The prevailing attitude there was a mixture of superstitious idolatry and enlightened philosophy. However, the things that others thought remarkable when they visited this city did not impress Paul. He had quite a different perspective – not because he was a philistine in cultural matters, but rather because he was a man totally focused on his calling. As Campbell Morgan describes it, "But all the man-made things he saw reminded him of man's capacity for God, and the degradation of that capacity".[8] While God can work with distressed and broken servants, he can do very little with indifferent ones.

● *A city full of idols.* In Athens, Paul was surrounded by the riches of four centuries of art and philosophy, with altars and temples all around him. A Roman satirist once said, "it is easier to find a god in Athens than to find a man". That about summed it up. The idols came in all shapes and sizes. They were made of stone, brass, gold, silver and ivory. Rarely have there ever been more options for worship. This sounds remarkably like the twenty-first century. We have to live in this environment, be aware of it and bring Christian testimony to many people who worship a multitude of God substitutes in one way or another. And many of these idols are associated with work or its products of wealth, success and ambition. As D.L. Moody wisely said, "Satan doesn't care what we worship, as long as we don't worship God".

Satan doesn't care what we worship, as long as we don't worship God

● *A lot of confused listeners.* Paul's message was for everybody. So we find him reasoning with Jews and God-fearing Greeks, then with the self-indulgent Epicureans and the cold, proud Stoics. The mix of people, philosophies and locations may be different in today's world, but the variety is similar – and so too is the confusion. The people did not give Paul's words a lot of credence. "What is this babbler trying to say?"[9] they asked, using the slang word for a seed-picker or a loafer who trades in scraps of learning. Not exactly an overwhelmingly positive response from his audience! On the face of it, it was not a good platform upon which to proclaim his message. Rather like the people of Athens, our work colleagues listen to lots of the latest ideas about the meaning of life – and they often see the gospel as only one contribution among many.

● *An unknown God*. Paul found an altar with this inscription on it, the very wording of which was itself an acknowledgment of their ignorance of this god. "Now what you worship as something unknown I am going to proclaim to you",[10] Paul declared. We have much to learn from Paul's tone here. He was not harsh or condemning; he noted their interest in religion and their evident need to worship; and he even quoted their own respected poets. He displayed both courtesy and kindness in large measure as he tried to build a relationship with his confused, yet learned, audience. Paul was clear that he had to bring the message of Christ, but he did it in a Christ-like way. If we could always remember that, people would receive our words so much better.

Paul was clear that he had to bring the message of Christ

● *A clear witness*. As he spoke to the audience on Mars Hill, Paul was tuned into God's purpose. The material he covers here is noteworthy, and a model of what we have to try to communicate – albeit often over a longer time scale and in various conversations. The antidote to idol worship (both then and now) was to tell them of the living and true God – as creator, sustainer, ruler, father and judge. But then came the crunch – as he fully discharged his responsibility to the Lord. "In the past God overlooked such ignorance, but now he commands all people everywhere to repent."[11] We often get to the point where people switch off and want to hear no more. Paul reached this point by mentioning the resurrection of the Lord Jesus. Such certainty was associated with judgment – and that is never popular. Ultimately people need to know the facts of the gospel.

● *A mixed reception*. Paradoxically, this reaction is encouraging for us. Some sneered, some postponed and some followed. At first glance, this was not a dramatic outcome – but the first response is not always indicative of the whole harvest. Indeed, in the case of Athens, church history tells us that there were subsequently excellent results from the preaching of the gospel in Athens. Those who sow seed have to learn to sow, and then wait. The verse from John Greenleaf Whittier sums this up to perfection.

> "Thine is the seed time; God alone
> Beholds the end of what is sown;
> Beyond our vision weak and dim
> The harvest time is hid with him"

☑ **ACTION:** You have walked through Athens with Paul and observed how he handled this opportunity. Use this framework to compare how you are handling similar situations at work. What have you learned from Paul? In what area do you most need God's help? We all need to pray that we will share Paul's attitude, "We proclaim him, admonishing and teaching everyone with all wisdom, so that we may present everyone perfect in Christ. To this end I labor, struggling with all his energy, which so powerfully works in me."[12]

How much progress am I making? One of the interesting characteristics of this militant secular age in which we live is the growing interest in the concept of "meaningful work". This concept implies that work should be both satisfying and something that calls for commitment, and that it should also give the worker a sense of wider purpose in his tasks. The cynic (or someone more interested in having a job than in metaphysical debate) might argue that any work that someone is willing to pay someone else to do must be meaningful. Yet many people are evidently looking for a dimension in their work beyond money – for some measure of autonomy and independence, for personal development opportunities, for ways of expressing their personality and so on. Part of this is finding a work environment that encourages, challenges and ensures that individuals give of their best. Christians readily relate to these desires.

More than that, Christians know the creator of "meaningful" work. God puts our work back into a right relationship with him, as expressed in passages such as "And whatever you do, whether in word or deed, do it all in the name of the Lord Jesus, giving thanks to God the Father through him."[13] The Bible is clear that the same God who has transformed us by his grace can extend this grace to all aspects of our life and work. Reflect on the specific work dimensions of this passage: "Therefore, if anyone is in Christ, he is a new creation; the old has gone, the new has come!"[14] This sounds like a radical new type of worker. Each of us needs to ask, "Am I that type of worker?"

The Lord intends that our joint work with him will be meaningful. But does it always feel that way? No, it doesn't. Do we always think that we are making progress in our witness to our colleagues? No, we certainly don't – unless your experience differs markedly from mine. Do we always have a feeling of job satisfaction in our work with the Lord? Sadly, not always – and sometimes there are long gaps between periods when we have that sense of satisfaction. Taking God into the workplace is a bit like moving up to the front line in a battle. Staying back in the reserves is a lot easier – but it does not fulfill our call. When we move forward we get closer to the enemy, and he can see us coming. Our intentions are clear to him, and his intentions should also be clear to us. We need to expect this battle and commit it to prayer. We sometimes forget to do that. We should never forget that it is only by engaging with the enemy that we get near those for whom Christ died. Neither should we forget that we are on the side of the victor! Alan Redpath's keen observation is very helpful here. "There is no winning without warfare; there is no opportunity without opposition; there is no victory without vigilance." The following, one of my favorite Bible verses, fills me with hope, gives me a great sense of the potential that God sees in each of us and leaves me breathless at the power of the risen Christ working through his people. "But thanks be to God, who always leads us in triumphal procession in Christ and through us spreads everywhere the fragrance of the knowledge of him."[15]

> *The Lord intends that our joint work with him will be meaningful*

It is in our nature to want to see progress – both in the short and long term. While God may allow us to see such progress, he may not. Chapters 3 through 7 have laid out some of the biblical prerequisites for progress –

both things to do and things to avoid. To be able to achieve the Lord's goals, we need to ask for the empowerment of the Spirit to apply these. While we are applying these truths, it is very likely that we will need to ask for double measures of patience, grace and love. We will also need to learn from each about different approaches to workplace ministry and seek to develop skills in this area. But, above all, we need to learn to listen to and respond to the promptings of the Spirit as opportunities are opened up to us. Paul was a person who was driven by goals. He uses an interesting phrase as he describes his own progress, "but I press on to take hold of that for which Christ Jesus took hold of me".[16] While Paul was pursuing Christ-likeness, he knew that he was not there yet and that there was much scope for improvement. We should ask the Lord to confirm why he "took hold of" us. William Barclay caught the thought behind these words beautifully when he said, "Every man is grasped by Christ for some purpose; every man is a dream of Jesus."[17] The Lord saw something in you and me that we may not yet have seen. May he use these pages to help us find that purpose and deliver on that vision of our potential. Since we often have many questions for God about our role in his work, we end this chapter with some encouragement from one of Paul's lessons to the church at Colossae.

Every man is grasped by Christ for some purpose

Asking questions, getting God's answers

"Let the peace which Christ gives settle all questionings in your hearts" (Weymouth).[18]

Following are some of the "questionings" that cross our minds.

● *Too good to be true.* Sometimes the very message of salvation by God's grace and Christ's sacrifice seems just that. "If God only knew what I was like" – but he does, and he always has. Remember, he chose the team. Think about the message that the angel gave to Zechariah – the good news that Elizabeth was to have a child, John the Baptist. Zechariah didn't believe it and was unable to speak until the words came true.[19] We have to believe God's good news in Jesus for ourselves and for others to whom we witness.

● *Too afraid to follow.* There are times when the challenges of the work environment are so daunting and the opposition so substantial that fear takes over. Jesus called Peter to leave the boat and follow, but the wind and the waves caused him to panic.[20] Jesus rescued him immediately – and queried his faith and weakness. He has to mount many similar rescue missions for us. He alone can keep us from losing our nerve – thus we learn lessons about heaven's buoyancy and earth's gravity.

● *Too weak to stand*. Most of us show weakness quite regularly. Listen to the ringing words of the prophet Jahaziel spoken to the king Jehoshaphat. "Do not be afraid or discouraged because of this vast army. For the battle is not yours, but God's ... Take up your positions, stand firm and see the deliverance the LORD will give you."[21] This advice occurs regularly throughout the Bible – precisely because we really need to hear and heed it. We need to stand firm in order for God to work through us. When we forget, we are much the poorer for so doing.

● *Too dark to navigate*. There are many times at work when we make this judgment call. The way ahead with people and situations is far from obvious. At times life could be said to be quite like Paul's commentary on a ship to Rome in very heavy weather. "When neither sun nor stars appeared for many days and the storm continued raging, we finally gave up all hope of being saved."[22] But Paul saw an angel who alleviated his fear, showed him the way ahead to Rome and gave him assurance of their survival. We, too, need promises and illumination – and both are available for the asking and for the believing.

Challenge No9

We have only touched on a few aspects of our lives in this chapter concerning whether or not our work is in line with God's plan. There are many other aspects to this question, some of which are considered in earlier chapters, especially Chapter 2. With all of what you have learned in mind, think and pray through the following issues.

1 Do you feel that you understand the consequences of your call to serve the Lord in your work?

2 Do you feel that you are equipped and ready to give an account of your faith to the different audiences you encounter at work?

3 If you were to choose one thing (above all others) that you wanted to put into practice regarding seizing opportunities in your workplace, what would that be?

4 Pray that God will help you to measure progress in your witness in his terms and empower you to respond to his timetable.

5 We all have unanswered questions about our Christian faith, not least because there are great mysteries underlying it. Pray that God will strengthen your grasp of the fundamentals and use this as a platform for witness through your work.

Further reading

Chalke, Steve, with Penny Relph, *Managing Your Time* (Eastbourne: Kingsway, 1998).

McGrath, Alistair, *Bridge-Building: Communicating Christianity Effectively* (Leicester: IVP, 1992).

Ortberg, John, *If You Want to Walk on Water You've Got to Get Out of the Boat* (Grand Rapids: Zondervan, 2001).

Roberts, Vaughan, *Distinctives: Daring to be Different in an Indifferent World* (Carlisle: OM Publishing, 2000).

Endnotes

1 This is a vital issue, considered in some detail in *Whose Life Is It Anyway?* (Carlisle: Authentic Lifestyle, 2002), Ch. 7, "Lordship, Grace and the Call of God".

2 Rev. 5:9-10.

3 1 Pet. 3:15.

4 Tit. 2:10.

5 Jas. 1:23-25.

6 Mark Greene makes a number of illuminating points on these issues in *Thank God It's Monday*, as do Michael Green and Alistair McGrath in *How Shall We Reach Them?*.

7 Acts 17:16.

8 G. Campbell Morgan, *The Acts of the Apostles* (London: Pickering & Inglis, 1946), p. 321.

9 Acts 17:18.

10 Acts 17:23.

11 Acts 17:30.

12 Col. 1:28-29.

13 Col. 3:17.

14 2 Cor. 5:17.

15 2 Cor. 2:14.

16 Phil. 3:12.

17 William Barclay, *The Letters to the Philippians, Colossians, Thessalonians* (Philadelphia: Westminster Press, 2nd edn, 1959), p. 82.

18 Col. 3:15.

19 Lk. 1:18-20.

20 Mt. 14:29-31.

21 2 Chr. 20:15-17.

22 Acts 27:20.

10
Weighing My Work in the Balance

"Now glory be to God! By his mighty power at work within us, he is able to accomplish infinitely more than we would ever dare to ask or hope."
(Eph. 3:20, NLT)

Outline The goals of this final chapter are to review what we have learned and to encourage you. While our past or present relationship with work may leave much to be desired, if we will apply these biblical principles to our work it will open up immeasurable potential for the Christian church. After tackling two important questions, we examine some matters to help us set a course for the way ahead.

Whose work is it anyway?: Conclusion
This opening section revisits the core question as it reviews central themes from the previous chapters and offers some conclusions. Our focus here is on the opportunities that God can open up through us, illustrated by the call of Mary's master at the resurrection.

Whose scales am I using?
There are three different scales we can use: namely our own, those of our peers, or God's scales. Using God's scales requires some spiritual exercise, and we see that several stumbling blocks are put in our way.

Setting the course for the way ahead
Some searching questions set out here help us to review our past and set a different course for the future. Out of this, we will explore some dimensions of a Christian's career based on Paul's writings to Corinth. Finally, we consider the matter of our will to please the Lord.

Whose work is it anyway?: Conclusion

We began our study of this question by acknowledging that this question is an awkward, difficult and demanding one. It is probably no less so now that we have reached the final chapter and can confirm that it is the Lord's work we do every day. Having accepted that we are indeed doing his work, we need to recognize and accept all of the help God gives us. We can do this by making this exciting theme text from Ephesians 3 our own. It's the "mighty power" that makes the glory possible.

If we surrender our work to him, God will achieve things through us that are way beyond our imaginations – outcomes that we would not dare to either ask or hope for. But there is a condition – I need to bring my work to the altar and lay it before the Lord. And we must live our lives in a way that will allow God's power to accompany us at work. Only then will it become God's work. Harry Emerson Fosdick said that "democracy assumes that there are extraordinary possibilities in ordinary people".

> *If we surrender our work to him, God will achieve things through us*

Christianity also makes that assumption. Jesus Christ knew that long ago, and it's the essence of this theme text from Ephesians. Remember that this is your work and mine that we are discussing – with all of its problems and challenges. God sees it as full of possibilities for his glory. This is not some ideal job in a uniquely favorable environment with especially receptive colleagues. It's none of these – it's the job you left the last time you closed the office, classroom, factory, surgery or bedroom door. It's the job with that unhelpful boss, the cynical colleagues, the unyielding client and the difficult customer. It's that job that fills you with anxiety, fulfillment, hope and frustration. That's the job that the Lord wants to join you in doing every day – thereby bringing glory to his name.

"Expect great things of God – attempt great things for God" was William Carey's great declaration of faith. Throughout the book, we have explored many different aspects of Bible teaching that are of relevance to the subject of work. The pages of this book have set out challenges and opened up the possibilities with passion and directness. Why? Because this is a major issue for the Christian church. But only God's Spirit can empower us to take these truths and apply them in each of our lives.

As we have seen, the answer to this central question involves much more than our lips. To make our work God's work we need to have changed attitudes in our hearts and we need to fully engage our minds and wills. Some of us need to set radically different patterns of behavior and new sets of priorities. All of this is counter-cultural and far removed from what many of us experience in our work environment. And this will be far from problem-free – quite the contrary. It is helpful to remember here the courageous words of Peter to a persecuted and despised group of disciples. "However, if you suffer as a Christian, do not be ashamed, but praise God that you bear that name."[1] In that environment, many people regarded the name "Christian" with contempt. There might be a higher general level of tolerance in our postmodern world, but the Christian's popularity is no more guaranteed, and many of our audiences are no less hostile at heart. As we face up to this challenge, it's worth recalling that the standard New Testament word for a member of the early church was not Christian, but "saint". This name had connotations of both holiness and being different – essential elements of our representation of the Lord, as we saw in Chapter 6. So to properly represent the Savior in our work, we will need to be firmly rooted and robust in our belief as to whose work it is. Table 10.1 summarizes some of the principal lessons of earlier chapters. In addition to being a useful review, this table might be used as a personal prayer list as we ask God to both reinforce the principles and enable us to implement them.

TABLE 10.1

Principles (Chapters 1 and 2)

Faith and work cannot be separated. To do so is to flaunt God's design for his people.

God presumes that our work involves us as co-workers, disciples with a calling, as we exercise stewardship of his resources and offer our work as a service. We do all of this in a way that brings glory to him.

My personal work is uniquely special to God – through it he expects me to be a witness, to be shaped to his ends as a person, to demonstrate his love and to bring glory to his name by my behavior.

Perspective (Chapter 3)

I will not understand whose work it is without having God's perspective on my work – all of us need to ask for this on an ongoing basis. God alone can give us this vital perspective.

To make sense of all the paradoxes of the work environment now and in the future, I need to find (and keep finding) stillness for deliverance, instruction and restoration.

Practice (Chapters 4-8)

The world of work holds particular dangers for Christians, and we need to recognize these. These dangers include being captured by the spirit of the age, failing to be a witness and regarding work as an idol to be worshipped. The antidote to all of these lies in a right relationship with God. Do I have one?

As we face up to the existence of conflict at work, we need to keep our (spiritual) eyes open. Conflicts with our colleagues will occur, and we need to handle them with grace and love. We also need to acknowledge and resolve conflicts with our owner on a daily basis.

God wants us to be his disciples at work, displaying integrity, character and the fruit of the Spirit. This is the best testimony that any of us could bring to our work. The mandate is to be salt and light and to engage in seed sowing. The challenge remains to ask what difference Jesus had made so far in our work – in our attitudes to people, work and morality and in our overall behavior.

Some aspects of our work take us to the moral edge. At all times, we need to respond to such challenges with the help of the Spirit as we find our way through the moral maze in matters of truth, respect for people, alertness of conscience, just behavior and practicing Christian love.

Many Christians feel excluded from the world of work and face different types of work-related crises – including finding work, staying in work, leaving work involuntarily and retiring. God does not exclude any of his disciples from his work, but those of us in regular, paid employment have a role to play in helping others who suffer from the discouragements that surround such work-related crises.

Progress (Chapter 9)

In order to make progress, I need to sense God's call and its consequences in my daily work. I need to tell my personal story of God's grace, and my behavior at work is the foundation for all my efforts to witness. The Lord looks for progress (and provides help for us) as we seek to create and take opportunities for witness. I need to honestly review just how much progress I am making in this area on a regular basis.

The missing link in all of the above is that each of us needs to hear the Lord call our name in order to make us personally aware of both the challenges and opportunities that stem from our work situation. Even in a family where there are many children, the father knows them all by name. He connects a task, advice or instruction to one of these children by using his or her name. So it is in the family of God. When, if ever, have you heard God's call by name? If you have, did it make you aware of a task that was yours and yours alone to accomplish? God calls us in diverse ways – through Scripture and advice from others; in times of praise and worship; through personal challenge from a preacher; in special circumstances of need and so on. The following is a biblical illustration of this personal touch, and its impact, when it comes from God. Although this is not a work-related scene, we have seen repeatedly that we need first to work on true discipleship and thereafter apply it to the work context.

Mary's master

The setting is the morning of Jesus' resurrection. The atmosphere is somber. Mary Magdalene, who owed so much to Jesus, is weeping at the tomb. There is a whiff of despair in the air, the tomb is empty and the cause is apparently lost. The disciples have dispersed, optimism and hope for the future are gone. The prospects for life ahead are grim, and persecution looms. Mistaking the Lord for the gardener, Mary asks where the missing body has been taken. With devastating effect, Jesus said to her "Mary".[2] What an extraordinary difference it made to hear that voice speak her name! Joy, triumph and pleasure overflow in her reaction – Jesus is alive! This difference has at least three dimensions.

● *The difference in the name*. He used her name, personally and exclusively. It stirred her memory, because she had clearly heard that voice before. Its tender use opened her eyes – the man at her side was definitely not the gardener. When she heard the unexpected voice, she was finally able to see what had been there to see all along.

● *The difference in the response*. Her formality goes and she responds in a very personal way because he was speaking to her alone. Her tears turn to joy and she feels new purpose, fresh direction and enlivened hope. She wants to grasp hold of Jesus and confirm the reality of his presence. She gets a fresh mandate, to go and tell his brothers, and she is reminded of a promise.

● *The difference in the news*. This is the heart of the matter. Jesus is no longer reported missing, his work stalled, his mission unfulfilled. Mary rushed to the disciples with the news "I have seen the Lord!".[3] Undoubtedly, this moment in Mary's life will hereafter be the key aspect of her story – the very foundation of her own witness. Few would query whose work Mary was doing after that experience! She now had the "good news" of the gospel. So do we.

Our contemporary setting is very different, but there are parallels in all three of these dimensions. Perhaps it has been some time since we listened for our name or recognized it when it was called. Maybe it has been even longer since we affirmed our response to it or took stock of the commitment we once made to spread the good news in and through our work.

☑ **ACTION:** As you have read this book and reviewed your own work situation, what have you identified as the biggest challenges in making your work the Lord's? Having read and prayed about the material in Table 10.1, what's the first step you now need to take to put your relationship with God and your work on a biblical footing? If you are already there and have put these principles into practice, think about ways in which you can mentor other Christians with regard to their approach to faith and work. Then go help them!

Whose scales am I using?   You have probably paused to think and take stock at many different points throughout this book, particularly in response to the challenges at the end of each chapter. In this final overview of our work-faith relationship, we need to ask whose scales and system of measurement we are using in our self-assessment. Three of the basic options include:

● *My own.* By this standard, you may be just fine. Work is deemed (by you) to be in balance with your faith and with all other priorities – that is, until you ask someone else (perhaps your partner or your family, or indeed your pastor, minister or vicar). Your own scales are good, high quality and durable – indeed, they may have lasted a whole (Christian) lifetime, without ever being at the repair shop for a service. Why? Because you designed them, built them and calibrated them, and you are their prime user. On their own they stand up, but read on …

● *My peers'*. By this standard, you may again seem in excellent shape – just because there are likely to be so many excesses in this reference group. In many cases this is like setting the hurdle level a few centimeters above the ground – getting over it is not a serious problem. Some of your colleagues may even think that a work-life balance is a new module on the multi-gym at the sports club. Others have no interest in achieving it and may even take pride in talking about it but never changing. It's a macho thing. But have you noticed that, if they are not Christians, their standard is automatically flawed? They have chosen not to be answerable to God. So their standards are not much use to you – even though you are tempted (or even at times obliged) to use them. And if you see Christian peers living according to their own standards rather than God's – and there are lots of them who do – don't copy them. Lift your sights higher. Don't go for the soft option.

● *My Lord's*. Now prepare yourself for a shock. The following are the standards for the citizens of heaven. It was Jesus who said, "If anyone would come after me, he must deny himself and take up his cross and follow me. For whoever wants to save his life will lose it, but whoever loses his life for me and for the gospel will save it. What good is it for a man to gain the whole world, yet forfeit his soul? Or

> *If anyone would come after me, he must deny himself and take up his cross and follow me*

what can a man give in exchange for his soul?"[4] Dietrich Bonhoffer, referring to discipleship, rightly commented that "salvation without discipline is cheap grace". The following four spiritual exercises, based on each of these four verses from Mark 8, are designed to help us reflect prayerfully on Jesus' profound and demanding words.

We are to deny ourselves as objects of worship – even as candidates for respect

(i) Listening (v. 34). What is Jesus asking? He is looking for an act of renunciation from each of us. We are to deny ourselves as objects of worship – even as candidates for respect. The positive action is, then, to shoulder our "cross" – with all its connotations of pain, disgrace and contempt. Jesus asks us to follow him – not in some general sense of offering service, but rather in the specific sense of imitation. Disciples follow masters.

(ii) Hesitating (v. 35). This so often describes our state of mind. To save our lives is to lose them; to lose our lives is to save them. Such is the paradoxical teaching of Christ. Losing our lives might involve losing literally everything, or not advancing in our careers, or radically switching our priorities, or something else altogether – but, if it is for his service, at his command and involves spreading the gospel, therein lies great gain. It is worth noting just how often this teaching about saving and losing features in the words of the Lord.[5] He clearly thought that it would be a major issue – and he was right! In order to make progress, we have to get past the hesitation stage.

(iii) Counting (v. 36). Here Jesus uses the language of ordinary secular business. What will be the surplus (or profit), applying the normal principles of value and exchange, even if the whole world, literally all that is material and visible, could be attained? This thought embraces all intellect, ambition, finance – everything that would attract us. And what's the potential loss? The soul is ruined and forfeited. In the rush and tumble of our work lives, much of which involves counting, this is one sum that we cannot afford to get wrong. We need to learn what to count and how to count it.

(iv) Thinking (v. 37). The final paradox is here in verse 37. It stretches to the incredible and sounds like a contradiction – "just suppose a man could give something for his soul". We know very well that there is no equivalent value – no one else could ever redeem it. No one, that is, apart from Christ the Lord. And it is he who calls us to give our work to him, because he has already redeemed our souls.

☑ **ACTION:** Reflecting on these four spiritual exercises will take some time and some peace and quiet. Try applying them to real situations in your life and working environment just to test the variance between the first two scales or standards (your own and those of your peers) and those of the Lord whose name you claim. Having done that, consider the weight of F.R. Maltby's remark, "Jesus promised the disciples three things – that they would be completely fearless, absurdly happy and in constant trouble".

As we ponder these words from Maltby and face the challenge of measuring our lives by the Lord's standards, we turn to consider Peter and John speaking before the Sanhedrin. This incident, as told in Acts, assures us that God can take ordinary people and enable them to do extraordinary things. Measured by the standards of the world around us, we may or may not feature in anybody's pecking order or be noticed by those in influential positions. While following the Lord does not guarantee us either one, neither does it exclude these possibilities. This passage is a great leveler. "When they [the Jewish leaders] saw the courage of Peter and John and realized that they were unschooled, ordinary men, they were astonished and they took note that these men had been with Jesus."[6] This text makes some interesting points about how people perceive us. John and Peter's backgrounds were not impressive, but their courage was. They were "unschooled" in the sense that they were not deemed qualified to engage in theological debate – that required rabbinical training – but they did know the presence of Jesus, and it showed! They were "ordinary" in that they had no standing in public affairs or noteworthy professional status. Their reason for being was simply expressed. "For we cannot help speaking about what we have seen and heard"[7] – back to the quality of their "story". William Barclay once said, "the most unanswerable defense of Christianity is a Christian man". Peter and

John's audience was astonished. How many people do we astonish with our witness and worship through our work and service?

The startling words from the pen of C.S. Lewis are worth considering here, "There are no ordinary people. You have never met a mere mortal ... But it is immortals whom we joke with, marry, snub, and exploit – immortal horrors or everlasting splendours". You might want to think about this statement as you reflect on what God can do with ordinary people. Ask him to give you insight into how he could use you to make a greater impact on others through your work.

We encounter many stumbling blocks in our paths as we try to apply this teaching to our work. Let me suggest three such stumbling blocks I have seen many times in my own experience and in observing others wrestle with their work. You might add others as well.

● *Milestones unobserved.* Many Christians don't quite know how they got into their present relationship with work – but they are very unhappy with it and know that their faith-work balance is not in line with God's plan. Was it one particular job or career change that brought them to this present state? Or working in an environment especially hostile to witness? Or were they influenced by peer group pressure? Was it not coping well with a new environment and new, strong-willed colleagues? Have they missed so many opportunities that they no longer know how to respond in a godly way? Was it a run of bad, unchristian behavior? Or a major personal moral failure? Whatever the balance of cause and effect, something crucial has happened – perhaps even by stealth – and it is difficult to undo its effects. The great message of the Bible is that you can start again – but doing this requires confession, will and courage. Learn, for example, from Peter's denial, David's moral failure and the frailty of Elijah.

> *The great message of the Bible is that you can start again*

● *Idols not burned.* We have observed in earlier chapters that work itself can become an idol, and that it can generate many attendant "mini-idols". During Paul's witness in Ephesus, Luke reports that "A number who had practiced sorcery brought their scrolls together and burned them publicly".[8]

This, and similar responses by new Christians, had a major impact on the way the word of the Lord spread in that city. You may not favor public burning, and our idols may have low calorific value – but we still need to let go of them if God is to use our work. We may need to participate in a very specific act of renunciation – perhaps concerning relationships, time-shaping priorities, behavior patterns or anything else that is the baggage of a past that we are supposed to have left for something far better. Each of us knows what our idols are.

● *Enemies not understood*. Work is such a blessing at one level, but we also know that it has its hazards. While work itself is not an enemy, we all wrestle with work at some time or another. And, for some of us, representing the Lord on earth through our work is a constant challenge. The following words should ring in our ears – even though many of us rarely think of them as applying to our work. "For our struggle is not against flesh and blood, but against the rulers, against the authorities, against the powers of this dark world and against the spiritual forces of evil in the heavenly realms."[9] There are definitely forces working against the Christian church taking the Christian message to the marketplace. We need to understand that it is a battle and daily equip ourselves accordingly. As Billy Graham said, "Jesus invited us not to a picnic, but to a pilgrimage; not to a frolic, but to a fight".

> ☑ **ACTION:** On balance, do you regard your present overall relationship with your work as a threat to, or as an opportunity for, Christian witness? Is that relationship consistent with what God asks of you? Honestly identify and assess your own stumbling blocks – and ask the Lord either to remove them or to remove you from them. Most of those listed above will only change at our initiative!

Setting the course for the way ahead Setting this course implies that we must undertake personal review and consideration and, above all, make choices. While we may be very constrained as to where we work and what we do, all Christians have a choice as to how we work. It often comes down to whether or not we are prepared to let Jesus Christ be the Lord of our work. I would be the last person to claim that integrating work and faith is easy. I have far too many bruises, I have let God down in too many situations, I did not seize the opportunity in too many incidents, and my behavior was not Christ-like in too many contexts to claim that. Yet I passionately believe that the fact that so many Christians (by their own confession) have a flawed faith-work relationship has created great damage to the advance of the faith – for all the reasons we have discussed. Too few of our colleagues have seen Christianity in action – we have introduced too few of them to Christ by our actions and words. This creates a new issue of stewardship – we need to be good stewards of our opportunities within an activity that takes up a great proportion of our lives. The personal question is, will your stewardship of this area of your life change? And will studying, knowing and praying about whose work it really is make a difference in your life?

God needs men and women who will powerfully represent him in the workplace and who clearly see that it is his purpose that they work for his glory where he has placed them. Gordon MacDonald has also wrestled with this problem of how to bring the kingdom of God to a place of work, and the questions he poses are very thought-provoking. As we reflect on what we have been learning together, we can all profitably ask them of ourselves.

- Are you maximizing your past experiences?

- Are you an asset or a liability?

- Are you managing the routines?

- Do you know which issues you are prepared to stand for, no matter what?

- Are you in a position to spread Christ-following values?

- What is the nature of your influence on key relationships?

- How do you handle your power and success?

- Are you maintaining life's balances?

- What do your spiritual disciplines look like?

- To whom have you made yourself accountable for personal and spiritual growth?

- Do you practice disciplined stewardship?

- Has your real-world faith helped some people to become Christ-followers?

- Where are you going?[10]

The Christian's career In order to look more deeply at these questions and root them in the Bible, we conclude by looking at the Christian's career through Paul's words in 2 Corinthians 1-5. Paul's words here reflect many issues concerning his Christian life and his apostleship, both of which were subject to some sharp criticism at the time he wrote this letter. This passage is a useful summary of many of the points that we have considered, and it also presents the challenge to apply what we have learned to our own specific circumstances.

☑ **ACTION:** Read 2 Corinthians 1-5.

- *Finding context.* While you may not think of it in these terms, every Christian has a career. When God called you, he guaranteed that you would have one. But you will have noticed how few secular careers go in straight lines. While there are people who do the job they were trained to do, and in the same place, for their whole working lives, they are few and far between. For example, many engineers become managers, lots of nurses become administrators and some classics graduates become merchant bankers! Only God knows the path that each of us will travel. In each individual's career there are both milestones and crossroads – times of critical and life shaping decisions. Sometimes these points of decision are obvious, while at other times changes around us subsequently affect us in ways we could never have predicted. You may be experiencing such a time of uncertainty as you read this book. I pray that it may help bring a new context to your life and work.

● *Setting targets*. Some people are very target-oriented. They have very clear career goals – expressed in terms of earnings, status, advancements by a certain age and so on. Indeed, for most of us, contemporary business and professional life is filled with goals and targets. It's possible that we know much more about our employer's objectives for us than we do about God's. If this is so, we need to lift our sights a little. Thinking of how he had survived in the past, Paul's advice was profound. "On him we have set our hope that he will continue to deliver us."[11] Much of what we have been discussing requires us to set additional (and perhaps very different) targets for our life at work. In order to achieve the goals that God has for us, we need to place our hope in him alone. But listen to the encouragement that comes with the call to be faithful. "For no matter how many promises God has made, they are 'Yes' in Christ."[12] Many years ago, I worked with a very wealthy and unhappy man. His family life was a mess, and he was very disappointed in his sons. He once told me that he would never trust anyone with his bank account. Yet God, through Jesus Christ, makes a totally open-ended commitment to us – to answer our core question, "Whose work is it anyway?", and respond in a Christian way to its implications, setting our targets with God.

> *Yet God, through Jesus Christ, makes a totally open-ended commitment to us*

● *Defining the job*. While God created each one of us with unique abilities and calls us to varying roles, he also equips us all with everything necessary to fulfill our calling as Christians. This passage points to several of these requirements for the Christian, one of which we touched on in Chapter 9. Namely, it is our responsibility that "through us spreads everywhere the fragrance of the knowledge of him".[13] A fragrance is a beautiful and appealing odor. We are also asked to show that we "are a letter from Christ"[14] – and to accept that this letter is open and read by all we meet. Whether we like it or not, as Charles Colson says, "Holiness is the everyday business of every Christian". Holiness is certainly a central requirement in the only version of our job specification that counts – the Lord's.

● *Seeking qualifications.* Some verses give us a lift – a sense that the Lord has been where we are before and knows all the issues that arise from trying to put into practice what we have been learning. The following verses impart just that sense. "Not that we are competent to claim anything for ourselves, but our competence comes from God. He has made us competent as ministers of a new covenant – not of the letter but of the Spirit; for the letter kills, but the Spirit gives life."[15] In addition to all the skills and energies that we bring to our working lives, we need this added gifting from God. By any standards, Paul was a highly trained man – but that was not enough in itself. Neither is it for us. And we need to be better at admitting that fact.

● *Being motivated.* Many aspects of every job are routine and lack glamor. We have all experienced them, and sometimes this dimension of our work diminishes our motivation. Tiredness and despair often follow. And our performance falters. Paul had his own share of pain with his mission – both physical and mental. He went as far as to say, "for I bear on my body the marks of Jesus".[16] While few can claim to parallel Paul's experience, most of us have an equivalent set of marks that remind us just how tough living for Christ can be. Paul's encouragement and motivation came from knowing that he had a mission to fulfill: "Therefore, since through God's mercy we have this ministry, we do not lose heart".[17]

● *Keeping real.* Status and position matter to people. Sometimes they matter too much – even to Christians who should know better. Paul's teaching here calls for a new level of humility – regardless of how much or how little we attain in the career stakes of this world. Some of the most arrogant Christians I have met are not those in positions of great authority in their careers, but others who have fallen in love with authority while in lesser positions – and who regularly abuse it. There is no scope for any of this in God's eyes. As Paul writes, "For we do not preach ourselves, but Jesus Christ as Lord, and ourselves as your servants for Jesus' sake".[18] The Servant-King himself calls Christians to servant status. As if to reinforce all of this and

The Servant-King himself calls Christians to servant status

reassure us, Paul then writes, "But we have this treasure in jars of clay to show that this all-surpassing power is from God and not from us".[19] Only God would link clay and power!

● *Maintaining perspective.* Various things cause us all to lose perspective at times – both in our daily tasks and in our Christian witness. Sometimes success and failure cloud our vision, or the apparently trouble-free lives of those who do not follow the Lord, periods of radical change and disruption, ill-health, family problems and so on. Paul notes that God's message of reconciliation has been passed to him and to all believers. If anything was ever designed to give us a proper perspective on how we all fit into God's plan, it's that very message. So, Paul concludes, "We are therefore Christ's ambassadors, as though God were making his appeal through us – we implore you on Christ's behalf: Be reconciled to God".[20] Of course, we need God's help to remember that and not to be overwhelmed by it. But, whatever we do, we must not hide from representing God as his ambassadors where we work.

A final word

God makes all things possible for us in Christ, but he needs us to do our part – not least to surrender our own will to his. As Frederick Wood wrote, "The will is the deciding factor in everything we do. In every sphere of life it settles alternatives". Indeed it does. I leave you with a poem introduced to me by my late father, whose testimony in his community and workplace always honored God. In that he showed me a fine example, and I am most grateful for that. I know that he would have found much to praise God for in this book – not least in its highlighting the potential for Christians to better link faith and work.

The will of God

My will is not my own
Till Thou has made it Thine
If it would reach the monarch's throne
It must its crown resign;
It only stands unbent, amid the clashing strife,
When on Thy bosom it has leant
And found in Thee its life

        – George Matheson (1842-1906)

Challenge No 10

1 Is your answer to our core question, "Whose work is it anyway?", any different now than when you started this book?

2 Take time to chart out the various twists and turns of your relationship with the world of work and the Lord of your life. Pray about the challenges that this assessment reveals.

3 After looking at the Christian's career through the biblical lens of 2 Corinthians 1-5, what do you need to review and reassess in your own situation?

Further reading

Griffiths, Michael, *Take My Life* (Leicester: IVP, 1967).

Hood, Neil, *Whose Life Is It Anyway?* (Carlisle: Authentic Lifestyle, 2002).

Silvoso, Ed, *Anointed for Business* (Ventura, CA: Regal, 2002).

Tozer, A.W., *The Pursuit of God* (Bromley: STL, 1982).

Endnotes

1 1 Pet. 4:16.

2 Jn. 20:16.

3 Jn. 20:18.

4 Mk. 8:34-37.

5 It is mentioned in all of the Gospels. See, e.g., Mt. 10:39; Lk. 17:33; Jn. 12:25.

6 Acts 4:13.

7 Acts 4:20.

8 Acts 19:19.

9 Eph. 6:12.

10 Gordon MacDonald, *Forging a Real World Faith* (Crowborough: Highland, 1989), pp. 266-70.

11 2 Cor. 1:10.

12 2 Cor. 1:20.

13 2 Cor. 2:14.

14 2 Cor. 3:3. This metaphor is developed in some detail in Hood, *Whose Life?*, Ch. 2, pp. 32-33.

15 2 Cor. 3:5-6.

16 Gal. 6:17.

17 2 Cor. 4:1.

18 2 Cor. 4:5.

19 2 Cor. 4:7.

20 2 Cor. 5:20.